346. 7304
TAL

DATE DUE

Commonsense Copyright

A Guide to the New Technologies

by

R. S. Talab

McFarland & Company, Inc., Publishers
Jefferson, North Carolina, and London

Library of Congress Cataloguing-in-Publication Data

Talab, R. S., 1948–
   Commonsense copyright : a guide to the new
technologies.

   Bibliography: p. 91.
   Includes index.
   1. Copyright—United States.   2. Fair use (Copyright)—
United States.   I. Title.   II. Title: Common sense
copyright.
KF2994.T36   1986   346.7304′82   85-43593
                       347.306482

ISBN 0-89950-224-5 (sewn softcover; acid-free natural paper) ∞

Printed in the United States of America.

McFarland & Company, Inc., Publishers
   Box 611, Jefferson North Carolina 28640

To my husband,
family and friends

Acknowledgments

The author wishes to thank the American Library Association and the International Council for Computers in Education for permission to reprint the following:

"Library and classroom use of copyrighted videotapes and computer software." Mary Hutchings Reed and Debra Stanek. © ALA, *American Libraries*, February, 1986.

Comments of the American Library Association on the Report of the Register of Copyrights to Congress: Library Reproduction of Copyrighted Works (17 U.S.C. 108), January, 1983. © ALA, 1983 (Appendix H).

International Council for Computers in Education (ICCE), *ICCE Policy Statement on Network and Multiple Machine Software.* ICCE, University of Oregon, 1787 Agate Street, Eugene OR 97403 (Appendix D). Permission granted to reproduce for educational purposes.

Table of Contents

Part II. Uses of Copyrighted Materials

Part III. Library Use of Copyrighted Materials

Part IV. Bibliography, References, Simplified Guidelines

Part V. Appendices

Foreword

This book is intended to clarify statutory law, related court cases, and legal opinion on common copyright and related legal aspects of print and nonprint acquisition and use. Its primary value is probably as a reference book: charts provided for various media should be consulted on most usage questions along with the appropriate text. Because copyright law is an area where experts disagree and circumstances change, consultation with a qualified attorney can always be recommended.

Part I

Introduction to Copyright

1
A Copyright Primer

Introduction

Interest in copyright and legal aspects of material use has grown enormously over the past few years. It is directly related to the increased ease with which materials can be produced and copied.[1] Electronic publishing, as Nicholas Henry stated in the prophetic *Copyright–Information Technology–Public Policy*, has influenced the politics of information access.[2] Not since the invention of the printing press has information technology influenced so many social and political changes.[3]

The photoduplicating machine, videocassette and videodisk players, cable television, the personal computer, the satellite, and the modem have enabled more people to have access to knowledge, information, and entertainment. For these reasons the balance between public access and individual rights has achieved greater importance.[4] It is now possible for an author to take a year to complete a work and anyone who is interested five minutes to duplicate it.

The introduction of these new technologies has enabled learning and invention to be spread more widely to the masses. The intriguing corollary of this dynamic arrangement is that proper remuneration should accrue to its creators.

Copyright Basics

Daily activities which involve the use of different media can be made easier with an introduction to some legal terms. Necessary to an

3

understanding of copyright is knowledge of its purpose, and area of coverage, and the differences among common law, statutory copyright, and agreements. These concepts provide a firm base for answering many copying questions.

Copyright. The copyright clause of the Constitution gives Congress the power to grant authors exclusive rights to their writings in order to "promote the progress of science and the useful arts" (Article 1, Section 8, Clause 8). The primary purpose of copyright is to foster the dissemination of intellectual works for the public welfare. Giving authors exclusive rights to their works for a limited period of time is seen as a way of rewarding them for their contribution to society.

"Copyright" literally means the exclusive right to make copies of a work. It could be described as a practical way of uniting publication with profit. By this method authors are given a "headstart" as a monetary incentive to creative production.

Since creative works are seen as a contribution to the public welfare, and the author's exclusive rights are designed so as to provide payment for this contribution, the problem of Congress was to foster dissemination of the works and yet not deprive the author of this incentive. Because of the need for balancing user and creator demands and the development of new technologies, the rights of authors are stated in broad terms in the new 1976 Act.

The scope of copyright has enlarged considerably over the years. The first United States Copyright Act was enacted in 1790.[5] (In fact, the first statute that Congress enacted could have been found guilty of copyright infringement. It was an almost exact copy of an earlier English statute.[6]) With later revisions of the act in 1831, 1870, 1909 and 1978, the scope of "writings" widened to include technological developments.[7] Now covered are literary, dramatic, and musical works, letters, maps, lectures, paintings, photographs, designs, sculpture, film, computer-readable databases, and computer programs.

Copyright does not apply to ideas. It applies only to their presentation—the actual arrangement of words, pictures, symbols, etc. For example, the theme or idea "boy meets girl" can't be copyrighted. But each unique story or expression of that theme can be copyrighted—*Romeo and Juliet, West Side Story, Oklahoma*, etc. Some degree of originality and creativity of expression is required, as well, for a work to be eligible for copyright.[8]

Statutory Law. Copyright law is governed by two aspects—statutory law and common law. They are of equal importance.[9]

Statutory law is enacted federal law. Federal copyright law (enacted by Congress) supersedes state copyright law. If there is a difference between the federal and the state law, then the federal statute takes precedence. What is not mentioned in a federal copyright statute devolves to state jurisdiction.[10]

Common Law. Common law is based on local customs as they are interpreted by the decisions of cases brought to the courts—court decisions. Statutory law is interpreted through court decisions. Some statutes require little interpretation because the law is simple or clear or because the area remains relatively static. Copyright law is an area which has experienced vast technological change so it requires a greater degree of interpretation by the courts.[11] Court decisions attain a high degree of importance in copyright law for this reason.

Agreements. Agreements, such as those negotiated by a Congressional committee for off-air taping, music, print, etc., have an impact on how the law is interpreted in future court decisions. There are various other agreements negotiated among interest groups, organizations, and associations, such as the Guidelines for the Educational Uses of Music or the International Council for Computers in Education (ICCE) Policy Statement on Network and Multiple Machine Software (see Appendix). When a case is brought to court, the judge examines any agreements or contracts between involved parties. While agreements apply only to those groups that negotiate them, they do provide a measure of guidance for interested users in two ways, by setting agreed-upon boundaries for the participating parties, and by aiding the courts in determining infringement should a dispute arise.

Contracts. A contract is a legally binding agreement.[12] While every contract is an agreement, not every agreement is a contract. The three elements that must be present are:

1. Consideration—a legal term for what one party to a contract gives to another. A contract could state that one party would pay the other party a certain amount of money for the purchase of a book, a software program, an article, etc.;
2. A time frame—the contract should specify the date of delivery, completion, or performance, and any starting or ending dates, if the contract is for a specific duration;
3. Signatures of all parties.[13]

Everything is negotiable in a contract, even copyright. While contract law and copyright law are distinct, a contract can assign or transfer copyright. For example, an author might transfer his or her copyright to a journal as a prerequisite to publication (this is not necessary, however; see section on copyright for writers). A software developer might assign one of the five "bundles" of rights, or any portion thereof, such as copyright or foreign distribution, to a company in exchange for royalties. The nature of the contract is an important consideration in copyright law.[14] (See Remer's *Legal Care of Your Software*: while the text is designed for computer software, the general information on contracts is worthwhile.)

Subject Matter of Copyright (101)

There are seven broad categories of copyright:

1. Literary works—books, periodicals, manuscripts, computer programs (including source code, programmable-read only memory chips, or PROMS, as well as support manuals and documentations), phonorecords, film, audiotapes, disks, and computer punch cards;
2. Musical works (including any accompanying words)—songs, operas, and musical plays;
3. Dramatic works (including music)—plays and dramatic readings;
4. Pantomimes and choreographic works;
5. Pictorial, graphic and sculptural works—fine and applied art, photographs, prints and art reproductions, maps, globes, charts, technical drawings, diagrams, and models;
6. Motion pictures and audiovisual works—slide/tape, multimedia presentations, filmstrips, films, videos, film loops, and film cartridges.
7. Sound recordings and phonorecords—disks, tapes, and cassettes.[12]

These categories overlap so that a motion picture may contain choreography and music or a computer program might have graphics or interact with a videocassette program, making more than one type of work which can be protected by copyright.

Ownership of Copyright as Distinct from Ownership of Material Object (202)

It is important to note that a distinction is made between the original work of authorship and the material object. For example, a book is not an original work, it is one of a number of copies.[13] The original work could be made into many types of copies—hardback books, paperback books, serializations in periodicals, audiotapes, phonorecords, video and computer disks, etc. Changing the manner of presentation of a work, such as from print to audiotape, does not change the need to follow the copyright guidelines.[14]

Duration of Copyright (302–305)

For authors, the best change in the 1976 Act was the lengthening of the copyright term. There were many reasons for this decision. Life expectancy has increased. Fifty-six years was not long enough to insure that an author and his or her dependents would realize adequate gain from a work. A term based on the year of death also greatly simplified copyright determinations. In this way, all the author's works would fall into public domain at the same time. Lastly, most of the other nations' participation in international copyright conventions had a term of life plus 50 years.

All copyrights now uniformly expire on the 31st of December, 50 years after the author's death.

The terms of copyright vary according to the type of authorship, the type of work, whether it was created before or after the 1976 Act, and whether the work is published or unpublished.

Basic Term—the life of the author plus 50 years for a work created after January 1, 1978 (302[a]).

Subsisting Copyrights—a work by a known living writer in a subsisting term of copyright at the time of the act has an extended period of protection. The term would be 75 years for works in their second term of copyright (28 for the first term and 47 for the second term). Works in their first term would be subject to the new act of the life of the author plus 50 years (304).

Joint Works—a work by two known living writers written after January 1, 1978, or in its first copyright term would be the life of the last living author plus 50 years, dating from the surviving author's death (302[b]).

Anonymous and Pseudonymous Works — the term of 75 years from the date of publication or, if not published, 100 from creation (302[c]).

Unpublished Works — unpublished works existing before January 1, 1978, are protected until December 31, 2002. If a work is published on or before December 31, 2001, then it is protected until December 31, 2027 (303).

Works for Hire — works produced after January 1, 1978, by a company or institution are copyrighted for 75 years from publication or 100 years from creation, which ever is shorter. In this category are all print and nonprint materials by corporate authors or companies, such as Warner Bros. film (101) (201[b]).

Compilations and Derivative Works (103)

A compilation is a collection of materials put together by an editor with an addition of annotations, introductions, supporting material, and criticism. In a compilation, only the *collection* of materials that the author chooses, their arrangement, and any contributions made by the compiler are copyrightable.

John Smith decides to compile a collection of poetry from 1900 to the present. He collects the poetry, arranges it, writes an introduction, annotates each of the poems, provides a brief critique of the poem, a background of each of the poets involved, and writes an index and bibliography. All publishers or authors whose poetry was copyrighted would have to be contacted to make arrangements for permission and payment (201[c]). This collection of poetry, including additions, would then be registered as a compilation.

A derivative work is one in which the new author adapts or transforms a previous work, making a new version of it. The author of a play, in this case, would grant permission to someone to make an adaptation for film or other media. For the work to be copyrightable by the person doing the derivative work, the derivative work must be made lawfully. All derivations must be made with the consent of the original author.

Uncopyrighted Works (102[b])

There are several kinds of materials which are not eligible for protection by copyright. There are also many kinds of materials for which copyright protection is not requested.

Works in the Public Domain. There are two types of public domain works—those for which copyright protection has expired and those for which copyright protection was not requested. When copyright protection has ended for a work it falls into the public domain.

There are no restrictions of any kind on the use of the work. Under the new copyright law works that ended their copyright protection before December 31, 1976, went into the public domain and the copyright cannot be retrieved. The law does not restore copyright.

The length of protection for works published under the old act was 28 years with a possible renewal period of another 28 years. However, under the 1976 Act, extensions for some of these materials increased the copyright for another 19 years, for a total of 75 years of copyright protection. Works published between 1910 and 1935 fall into the public domain each year (1910 + 75 = 1985). Works published later than 1935 fall under extended copyright protection (304).

Public domain works for which copyright protection was not requested may be freely used, also. There will not be a copyright symbol on the work, and in most cases, there will be a statement that the work is public domain. The most common example of public domain work is the computer program listed in a journal or hobbyist magazine which may be input for personal use.

Ideas, Methods, Systems, and Principles. Copyright does not apply to ideas, methods, systems, principles, processes, concepts, etc. The "theory of relativity" can and should be used by anyone wishing to apply it in an article or book. In the educational context, concepts such as "accountability" and "computer literacy," or other such ideas, are free to be used by anyone regardless of whose original idea it was. What can be copyrighted is the presentation of the idea—in a book, article, game, or whatever. People purchase the presentation, not the idea. The idea may be used freely.

Common or Standard Works. Works which contain no original authorship can be freely used. Standard calendars, height and weight charts, tape measures and rulers, and lists of tables taken from public documents or other common sources are not subject to copyright protection. What can be copyrighted is the method of presentation. A growth chart for children consisting of height measured in inches, with each foot depicting a taller animal with a special saying and with artwork would be a unique presentation subject to copyright. The concept of a ruler is not.

Devices and Blank Forms. Devices for measuring or computing, or for use in conjunction with a machine are not subject to copyright protection. Slide rules, wheel dials, nomograms, mathematical principles, formulas, equations, and devices based on them are not copyrightable. The printed material of which a device usually consists (lines, numbers, symbols, calibrations) cannot be copyrighted because the material is necessary for the idea, principle, formula, or standard of measurement involved to be used. Blank forms, or any forms designed to record rather than to convey information, cannot be copyrighted, either.

Deminimus Works. Certain kinds of works are not considered important enough for copyright. These are works in which the creative authorship is very small.[15] In these cases the legal maxim "de minimus con curat lex" (injury not sufficiently serious to warrant judgment) applies.[16]

Slogans, titles, names, variations or typographic ornamentation, lettering or coloring, etc., are not copyrightable. The use of slogans and trademark names, such as "Coca-Cola," in a nonprofit context does not present a problem unless someone sold a homemade drink and called it "Coca-Cola." Trademarks are protected by patent and trademark law. This law is designed to keep someone from using a name in order to profit from a product that is not authentic or that damages a product in the eyes of the public.

Works of the United States Government (105). Works produced by the U.S. Government cannot be copyrighted. This applies to unpublished works as well as published ones. Section 409 also provides that when a U.S. Government work has been republished commercially and new work is added, such as an introduction, illustrations, and explanations, etc., only the material added is copyrightable by the new contributor.

Moreover, the notice must identify those parts of the work which are not copyrighted, when a work is "preponderantly" that of the U.S. Government. The only exception is that of the National Technical Information Service, which may have a limited copyright of up to five years.[17]

New Versions

New versions of works are those in which material is added to an existing work. The copyright in a new version of an existing work covers only the new material. The addition of the new material does not change the expiration date of the original material to which the new material was added.[18]

Rights of the Copyright Owner (106)

There are five separate and exclusive rights which are granted to the copyright owner, each of which may be transferred separately or jointly. They are:

1. Reproduction—the right to reproduce the first or original embodiment and any copies;
2. Preparation of Derivative Works—the right to produce a new version of the author's work. Derivative works include translations from one language to another, including computer languages, musical arrangements, dramatizations, fictionalization, motion picture adaptations, sound recordings, art reproductions, abridgments, condensations, or any other form in which the work is altered or adapted.
3. Public Distribution—the sale, gift, or other transfer of ownership, rental, lease, or lending of the author's work. If an owner chooses to sell a publisher the manuscript, then the right of public distribution is sold so that copies of the work can be distributed. In this type of transfer, the author generally contracts to be given certain royalties on the sale of the work to the public. Types of distribution, such as hardback and paperback rights and foreign distribution, are contractual.
4. Public Performing Rights—literary, musical, dramatic, and choreographic works, pantomimes, motion pictures, and other audiovisual works. The following would constitute a performance of a work: live renditions that are face-to-face, renditions from recordings, broadcasting, retransmission by cable, microwave, etc. To "perform publicly" is defined as a performance at an establishment open to the public or where a substantial number of persons outside of a normal circle of a

family and its social acquaintances is gathered. This definition makes performing in a not-for-profit environment, provided that the performance is not open to the public, like a reading, a demonstration, or a play. If tickets are sold, then it is considered a for-profit use open to the public, and it is clearly a violation of the author's rights.

5. Public Display—to display a work by means of film, slide, television image, or any other type of device. Motion pictures and other audiovisual works are considered exhibitions rather than displays. Public display applies to any work embodied in a manuscript or printed matter, and in pictorial, graphic, and sculptural works, including "stills."[19]

Some new distinctions between the rights of the author and the user have been made and they affect copyright ownership.

Author as Source of Copyright Ownership

The source of copyright ownership is the author of the work.[20] Any work by an author in which ownership can be proven has copyright protection whether published or unpublished. Before the 1976 Act a work could not be copyrighted until it was published and there were several criteria to be met for a work to be considered legally published. Under the 1976 Act, the author's work is eligible for copyright protection from the time it is written or recorded. Upon publication of a work the author may elect to keep the copyright or transfer distribution, public performance, or other rights individually or collectively.

Federal Preemption of Common Law Copyright (301)

Common law copyright is preempted and a single federal system of statutory protection is established for all works, published and unpublished. Works not considered published, and thereby not subject to statutory copyright protection, such as speeches, letters, theses, dissertations, manuscripts, and other historical material are protected by federal law. They are also subject to fair use.

Works for Hire (101) (201[b])

A work for hire is a work written by an employee or contractor within the scope of employment. In such a case the copyright is owned by the person or entity who hired the employee to produce the work.

When a work is commissioned by an institution, rather than produced within the scope of work activities, then a written contract should be signed by the parties stating the purpose of the work commissioned by the institution and the rights and obligations of the author and the institution.[21]

If an independent author, whether of a book, audiovisual work, song, computer program, etc., contracts with a company or institution to produce a work, whether or not the resulting work will be a "work for hire" depends on the type of contract. If the independent author signs a contract that the resulting work is a "work for hire" then the independent author does not retain copyright. The company or institution would retain the copyright because the agreement stipulated that this was to be so.[22]

Notice of Copyright (401)

Section 401(b) states that the notice of copyright must have three elements:

1. the symbol © (the letter c in a circle), or the word "copyright," or the abbreviation "Copyr.";
2. The year of the first publication of the work, or when completed (if unpublished).
   a. for compilations or derivative works incorporating previous work, the year of first publication is sufficient;
   b. The year date can be omitted where a pictorial, graphic, or sculptural work, with accompanying text matter, if any, is reproduced in or on greeting cards, stationery, jewelry, dolls, toys, or any useful articles; and
3. The name of the owner of a copyright, or an abbreviation by which the name can be recognized, or a generally known alternative designation of the owner.

The position of the copyright notice has to "give reasonable notice of the claim of copyright" (Section 401[c]). In essence, the notice shouldn't be put in an inside corner in the back of a book or in a difficult to locate position on a work.

Fixation (102)

The most basic concept change in the copyright law is that of fixation.[23] Any work has copyright protection eligibility the minute it is recorded. This does not mean that copyright protection is assured even though a work has not been registered with the Copyright Office. In order to be eligible for certain remedies a work must be registered (412). Registration is the best legal protection; should litigation arise over the question of authorship the work is only thereby legally secured. Fixation is a device to ensure that both published and unpublished works are protected by federal statute whether the form is in words, numbers, notes, graphic or symbolic indicia, etc. In this way a computer program, an audiocassette tape, a videocassette program, etc., are all eligible for the same copyright protection.

Contributions to Collective Works (201[c])

Contributions to collective works (periodicals, books, anthologies, compilations, etc.) are copyrighted by a journal, for example, as a collection. The individual copyright on the separate work may be retained by the author, so that the author does not need to transfer his or her copyright in order for the work to be published. There are two possible copyrights — one for the individual contributor and one for the collection.

Registered Mail as "Poor Man's" Protection

Writing a song, poem, story, computer program, etc., then sending it to oneself via registered mail and keeping it sealed has been a commonly held idea for copyright protection. It is sometimes called the "poor man's contract." If an infringement case ever went to trial, the plaintiff (who sent the registered letter) could introduce the sealed package as evidence of ownership. This would require the court to be convinced the mail was not tampered with (hard to prove) and also that it was properly mailed. The court would have to rely on the plaintiff's testimony; in addition, none of the benefits of Copyright Office Registration would be available to the plaintiff. (See page 57.)[24]

While some authors believe that separate registration is too costly if the author has, say, several songs, the fact is that several works may be registered together as a collective work, thereby saving multiple registration charges.

Infringement (501–510)

To "infringe" copyright means to violate any of the five exclusive rights: reproduction, preparation of a derivation work, public distribution, public performance, and public display. An infringer could unwittingly violate one or more of the copyright owner's rights. For example, if a theater director bought one copy of a play, reproduced several copies for the cast, and later performed the play for the public without paying performance royalties and charged admission, then the director would be guilty of two separate violations, reproduction and public performance.

In pursuing an infringement suit, the copyright owner could choose two avenues — actual damages, including additional profits made by the infringer, or statutory damages (504).

If the owner elected to receive actual damages, then the costs of copies of the play distributed to cast members by photocopying, the royalty for the number of nights that the play was shown, and perhaps all or a percentage of the profits that the play took in could be requested as damages, and a fine could be imposed.

If statutory damages were chosen, then the copyright owner (plaintiff) could elect to recover from $250 to $1,000 per offense. However, if the violation involved large amounts of money or widespread usage, the court could award from $100 to $25,000 per offense, but not more than $50,000 total.

Court costs and attorney's fees could be awarded at the court's discretion (505). If the defendant lost, he or she could be ordered to pay court costs and attorney's fees for both sides. Time lost due to court appearances can be a major consideration. In most cases, the institution or business would be named as co-defendant in the suit. In addition, the employee or corporate officer could also be liable for contributory infringement.[25]

The "Innocent Infringer" Provision (504[c][2])

Help for nonprofit users in the form of the "innocent infringer" provision was widely discussed before its adoption in the new law. It was designed to provide broad insulation for the teachers, librarians, archivists, public broadcasters, and the nonprofit institutions of which they are a part.

In the case of the "innocent infringer" (someone who honestly believed that the act was not a violation of copyright, and had no good reason to believe otherwise), the fine can be waived. In these cases, the "burden of proof" would be on the defendant. He or she would be required to prove his or her good faith and innocence of any wrongdoing.

Part II
Uses of Copyrighted Materials

2

Fair Use

The fair use doctrine, codified for the first time in Section 107 of the 1976 law, is nearly 150 years old.[1] It can be defined as a public usage for which the copyright owner is not remunerated, presumably because it is minimal and because it is in the public interest. The primary concern is with the promotion of the public interest, which is accomplished through the balancing of the "dissemination of knowledge with the negligibility of use."[2] Copyright authority Saul Cohen, in perhaps the definitive expression of what constitutes fair use, expressed the feeling of the courts:

> This is really a pretty trifling and insignificant thing the defendant has done; he acted reasonably, he meant no harm, he has not profited greatly and the plaintiff is not really hurt; so, we will not find any infringement by this use.[3]

Fair use was developed as all judicial doctrines are, by precedent. Historically, it has developed from a little-used defense in infringement cases to a widely-accepted doctrine of important use and scope.[4]

The doctrine draws its substance from the same constitutional clause as copyright, because it is believed to be necessary in order to "promote the progress of science and the useful arts."[5] This concept was evident in the first copyright act of 1790.[6] It was called "An act for the encouragement of learning...."

The doctrine has been allowed to grow because of the belief of the framers of the Constitution that the granting of copyright was for the purpose of the public interest or the public good.[7] While each case is different, complicated computations with each usage was not what the law intended. Responsible use requires some knowledge, some consideration, and a practical, flexible policy.

The Four Criteria

The thrust of the four fair use criteria is most often found to be economic.[8] However, each of the four criteria are important in fair use considerations.[9] An understanding of how these four factors tend to be evaluated is essential.

The answer to the question "how can I comply with the law?" is often just common sense.[10]

It is important at this point to remember that a case comes to court because there are two sides to an issue. This is why some reasoning should be applied to usage, particularly with magnetic media, such as computer software, videodisks, and the like, because these areas of developing technology await clearer definition of the parameters of fair use.[11] Circumstances change; however, the basic rationale has remained essentially the same.[12]

The four factors of the fair use doctrine act as weighted measures.[13] In some cases the purpose of the use would be sufficient to make a use unfair. In another situation, the amount of the use, while small in quantitative terms, might be so qualitatively essential to a copyright owner's market that such a use could harm the potential market of the author. Each of these four factors should be considered in using both print and nonprint materials.[14]

(1) *Purpose and character of the use*—how the material is used, such as for profit or nonprofit purposes, and the intent for which it was made.

Profit use of a profit work is most liable for a suit. A nonprofit use of a profit work would depend more on the particular circumstances of the use.[15]

(2) *Nature of the copyrighted work*—this is the expectation of the author and society on its value and usage, as well as whether or not the work is scholarly or commercial.[16]

The most common distinction for usage purposes is if the work is scholarly/informational or commercial. If the work is scholarly, then the expectation of the author and publisher would be that the work would be used for educational or research purposes. While the author isn't generally paid, and often must pay for defraying the cost of publication in some fields, such as psychology, it is a professional courtesy to request permission for uses over the guidelines. Historically, fair use of scholarly/informational work is accorded greater protection. Permission requests gauge the acceptance of the author's work professionally and in some cases are part of the merit system of an institution.

The expectation of an author who writes articles for *Atlantic Monthly*, *PC World*, or produces films or music, etc., is that fair use will be made of the work in the nonprofit/educational context and that the work will not be substantially used by another writer to make a profit.

The exception is producers who create profit works for the educational market. For educators to use these works, the very audience to whom the materials are directed, without payment or permission would be detrimental to their market, since the work is designed to sell to educators.

(3) *The amount and substantiality of the material used*—that is, how much of the work is used, both qualitatively and quantitatively.

Amount is an important factor in using most print materials.[17] The substantiality of a work is considered in terms of how important the portion used is in relation to the work as a whole and is important in music, for example. A line or melodic phrase could be the identifying or key part of the song. A particular algorithm could be the key to a certain type of program. While amount is usually considered to be length, substantiality is a qualitative judgment and is concerned with the importance of the amount taken in relation to the entire work.[18]

(4) *The effect of the use on the potential market of the work*—this involves an estimate of the expected purchasing audience of the work. While all the rest of the factors deal indirectly with economics, this criterion deals specifically with this aspect, either in actual or estimated market loss.[19]

The Three Fair Use Tests

Copying, whether using photoduplicating machines, videocassette recorders or microcomputers, is the heart of the fair use issue. The three tests as described in the *House Report*—brevity, spontaneity, and cumulative effect—are directed toward illustrating the parameters of these uses that are generally considered fair.[20]

(1) *Brevity*—this controls the relative amount of what is copied: 250 words for poems, 2500 words or 10 percent of articles, stories, etc., as given in the fair use charts for various types of print and nonprint materials uses.[21]

(2) *Spontaneity*—for a work to be considered spontaneous it must not be calculated enough ahead of time that reprints or permission could be acquired. This criterion is designed to capture the "teachable" moment when something is needed for the classroom immediately. It also controls the intent in making copies and emphasizes responsible use and "good faith."[22]

(3) *Cumulative effect*—this is an aggregate use, the combination of small uses that become additive to such a proportion that continued copying could or would harm the potential market for an author. Cumulative effect is the result of many one-time unauthorized uses of a chapter of a book or an off-air tape, for example, across a large district, college, company, or other institution.[23]

Because this test is the most difficult to evaluate, what is required is that someone, whether in the library, audiovisual department, copy center, or elsewhere, take an overall look at the copying practices of the institution. More than one court case has involved an abuse of this test.

3

Print Materials

Educational Guidelines for Nonprofit Copying

The "Agreement of Guidelines for Classroom Copying in Not-For-Profit Educational Institutions" (see Appendix A) was directed to nonprofit and educational institutions at all levels. They were hammered out by the Ad Hoc Committee on Copyright Law (representing many educational associations) and two author-publisher groups.

The guidelines were meant to be stated as a "reasonable interpretation of the minimum and not the maximum standard" for use.[1] The guidelines were not designed to be punitive. They were drawn in accordance with the policies of a large number of authors and users for the majority of instances.[2] They provide a standard for usage—one that had not been provided before.

Some changes in the Copyright Act helpful to educators and other nonprofit users are:

1. No restrictions on the number of articles or number of times that newspapers, current news periodicals, and current news sections of other periodicals can be copied for a "course."[3]
2. Single copying for purposes of instruction and research is now legally permissible by statute.[4]
3. Multiple copies for classroom use is sanctioned for the first time in the new law.[5]
4. Fair use parameters have been codified into law for the first time (Section 107).

Chart A on page 114 provides a simplified interpretation of usage for print materials. Certain works are prohibited from fair use. These are: workbooks, study guides, manuals, and standardized tests and test booklets.[6] In addition, copying of a number of poems, stories, etc., should not substitute for an anthology.[7]

Reproduction of Print Material — Usage Examples

Examples of usage for print, special print, and nonprofit materials are provided alphabetically within these categories. When more than one type of material is listed, the use must be treated the same for all types listed in that category; for example, essay collections, anthologies, and encyclopedias are listed as one category and their use is the same.

(1) *Architectural drawings* — an instructor makes an overhead transparency of a drawing from a book of drawings that she is using in her class. ***Yes.** Leave designer's name on the transparency.

(2) *Children's books and "special works"* — to illustrate a point in story telling, a photocopy is made of a page of the children's book being discussed for each student in the class to evaluate. ***Yes.** Special works can be children's books or any work which combines a comparatively small amount of prose and many illustrations, such as Shel Silverstein's *The Giving Tree.* Any such work with 2,500 words or less qualifies as a "special work" and only 10 percent may be used.

(3) *Encyclopedias and anthologies* — two essays, totaling 3,000 words, are reproduced from a current encyclopedia volume. These essays are then distributed to students in a creative writing class. ***Maybe.** The general rule for excerpts from this type of material is 2,500 words in an excerpt or essay. This amount exceeds the guidelines, though not to a great degree. The *House Report* notes that there may be instances which legitimately exceed the guidelines; however, caution is advised.

(4) *Government documents* — for soil testing information, several pages are taken from a U.S. government pamphlet, photocopied, and are distributed to students to keep. There was no copyright mark. ***Yes.** Government pamphlets are free to be used. The only exception would be if there was a copyright mark — ©. This generally means that the work was contracted and given copyright. Fair use rules would have to be followed. With the exception of publications of copyright term from

the date of publication, government documents, pamphlets, books, etc., are nearly always copyright free, and may be freely copied.

(5) *Lectures, sermons, speeches*—a history instructor wishes to photocopy an 1100-word speech of Alfred North Whitehead for a unit on World War II. The speech is in a collection of published speeches found in the library. It will be distributed to a history class. ***Yes.** Fair use can be made of speeches found in a published work. Unpublished speeches, lectures, and sermons existing before January, 1978, not yet in the public domain are protected for the life of the known author plus 50 years. However, even for works under the new law for which the life plus 50 term has expired or would expire soon, all common law works are protected until 2002.

(6) *Maps, charts, graphs, cartoons*—to illustrate the change in political maps for a class, the instructor takes two maps out of textbooks and periodicals to make overhead transparencies for class. ***No.** The rule for these materials is one per issue or one per book. However, if the use was spontaneous the circumstance would be different.

(7) *Newspapers, current news sections of periodicals*—for a current events project, the students in Instructor Y's class are allowed to keep a notebook on some aspect of world affairs. At the end of the unit, each student will copy the materials in the folder and distribute them to their classmates. All the students will then have a bound folder for further reference during the next two units. ***Yes.** Both newspapers and current news sections of periodicals are subject to free use—any amount can be legally copied for any purpose.

(8) *Novels, nonfiction, textbooks, theses*—in a current-trends-in-fiction class, students are encouraged to copy 250-word, one-page excerpts from the novels that they are studying on their own. These excerpts are collected and distributed to other members of the class. Four excerpts are required for criticism and comment. ***Yes.** A 1000-word excerpt is allowed twice per class per term. Four 250 word excerpts, while not in line with the cumulative rule, add up to the amount rule for term use. Other copying should be curtailed. On the other hand, one 2000-word excerpt takes more from an individual author, and therefore could potentially do more harm; so more caution would have to be used in taking a larger amount from an individual author than small amounts from different authors.

(9) *Photographs, pictures*—to illustrate different kinds of Pacific Northwest flora, a biology instructor makes two transparencies from a

current periodical that has pictures of various kinds of plants. ***Yes,** as long as the photographs are not individually copyrighted. If there are copyrights on the pictures, then this means that each picture is individually copyrighted. In that case, none of the pictures could be used without permission.

(10) *Poetry*—for a modern poetry section, an instructor makes photocopies of small portions of song lyrics in four cases and of two entire songs in order to illustrate rhyme schemes. The entire songs that were used were made into transparencies for one-time classroom use. The smaller portions of songs were used as portions of test questions for a quiz. ***Yes.** The entire songs were not distributed to the class, and the number of songs used for transparencies was small. Multiple copies of entire songs should not be made. Using only a small amount of each song would put the use within the guidelines if treated as lyrics only. If the instructor used more than a small amount, or used a complete song and passed several of these songs to students to use, then it would be considered unfair use. If, on the other hand, students were encouraged to bring one or more copies of songs that they had chosen individually for study and comment, this would be better because one author's song has not been distributed to an entire class.

(11) *Short stories, essays*—two stories, totaling 7,500 words, are taken from a living writer's story collection. These essays are then distributed to students in a creative writing class. ***Yes,** two essays are fine to use, as long as the cumulative rule of two per class per term is observed. The general rule is a 2500-word excerpt or story, although this may vary according to the "spontaneity" test. However, 7,500 words is a fair amount of paper and clearly exceeds the guidelines. Using reprints would be wiser, both in terms of time and expense.

(12) *Works copyrighted prior to 1907.* In order to demonstrate Victorian literature in England (circa 1876–1879), an instructor copies a chapter out of three popular works of the period and distributes them to the class for discussion and comment. ***Yes,** works by known authors copyrighted prior to 1907 will have the first term of 28 years expired and any possible renewal period of extension expired, as well. Works copyrighted from 1907 to 1935 will have copyright terms of 75 years. These works began falling into the public domain in 1982. For example, a work written and copyrighted on January 15, 1926 will go into the public domain on January 16, 2001 (26 + 75). Works published after 1935 are subject to the new copyright term of the life of the author plus 50 years.

Special Categories in the Educational Setting

Student Publications

Campus student publications, such as the newspaper, literary magazine, etc., should follow the fair use guidelines closely. If these publications are sold, then greater care should be used. Occasionally, there are cases involving infringement in student publications, generally involving the newspaper, so faculty advisors should make sure that fair use is followed.[8]

The liability of the school for the content of the publications of its students is largely dependent on the relationship of the institution to the publication. If the publication is featured as part of a school or university activity, if it is supported by the institutional treasury, and if the institution has the right to review articles, then the university or school's liability for what is printed there is increased. Student editors should be instructed that quotes of a substantial part of a work should require permission, which will generally be granted with a fee.

Textbooks and Works of Faculty Members

Where the line should be drawn between a work undertaken as a college or university responsibility and one that is a private endeavor is a question of both philosophical and practical consequences and workable policies are needed.[9] Works by faculty under agreement between a school or college are considered "works-for-hire" (see page 13). In the absence of such an agreement, and if the instructor undertakes the work on his or her own time, all such works are the property of the instructor. For specialized research the agreement should be in writing.[10]

The right of instructors and those performing duties in connection with a school or college to copyright their works, including lecture notes and manuscripts, has been well defined by the courts.[11] Works produced by educators on their own time and not a part of assigned duties are their own. Even if the work is printed or published by the school or government or governmental facilities have been used in producing the work it would not entitle the institution or the government to any literary rights. The deciding factor is whether or not an agreement was entered into by the instructor and the institution for the purpose of producing the work. (See page 13.)

Photocopying in the College and University

The role of the university is that of vanguard, forming the "cutting edge" of intellectual advancement. Because of higher education's greater need for up-to-date materials, the formulation of the guidelines for educational copying caused some concern in higher education.[12]

The *House Report 94-1476*, which contained the guidelines, addressed this concern. The *Report* noted that the Association of American University Professors and the Association of American Law Schools had written the committee "strongly criticizing" the guidelines as being too restrictive for classroom teaching at the university and graduate level.

In reply, the *Report* reaffirmed that the purpose of the guidelines was to state the "minimum and not the maximum standards" of educational fair use and that the agreement acknowledged that "there may be instances in which copying which does not fall within the guidelines ... may nonetheless be permitted under the criteria of fair use. The committee believes the guidelines are a reasonable interpretation of the minimum standards of fair use."[13]

The elasticity of the guidelines, particularly in the college and university setting, was clarified, The Ad Hoc Committee replied:

> The guidelines are intended as a "safe harbor," assuring the teacher who stays within their scope that he or she will not be liable for infringement. They do not speak at all to the possible additional uses that are still protected by the fair use doctrine.... In short, there is potentially a great deal of educational photocopying beyond that set forth in the guidelines that will clearly be lawful in the future as it has been in the past.[14]

Higher education has a greater need for current material, and this need is part of its mission. Consequently, the guidelines are intended to be interpreted with some degree of flexibility.

Campus photocopy centers must adhere to strict copyright guidelines. Publishers have been known to send a representative to check a center's copyright compliance anonymously.

Copyright Clearance Center

The Copyright Clearance Center (CCC) is a nonprofit organization established in 1971 by authors, publishers, and users of copyrighted material. The CCC conveys after-the-fact authorizations for photocopies made by users of copyrighted material. Royalty fees are set by publishers and authors and the CCC handles royalty fee collection and distribution with a small added service charge. There are currently 11,500 journal and book titles (but mostly journals) and 1,100 publishers registered. Users are from organizations, academia, and government. Its services include a Document Delivery Awareness Program, which links publishers and documents suppliers with users, the reciprocal agreements that are being established with royalty collection agencies in foreign countries, and several publications, many of which are available at no charge. Their address is: Copyright Clearance Center, Inc., 21 Congress Street, Salem MA 01970, 617-744-3550.

4
Nonprofit Uses of Music

In many ways the "Guidelines for Educational Uses of Music" (see Appendix B on page 122) is like that for print materials. Classroom uses of music and certain types of performances are still exempt, but the law now has a narrower definition of "nonprofit" uses than did the 1909 Act.[1] In practice, it had not been necessary under the old law for schools to secure rights to give performances of nondramatic musical works (this excluded plays and operas) and the new law is the same. However, if admission is charged at a nonprofit performance, the proceeds must only be used for educational or charitable purposes.[2]

As with print materials, one may make a copy of a performable unit (movement, aria, etc.) for personal or nonprofit use and multiple copies may be made for classroom use of a small amount of any performable unit. The one exception to copying is the emergency performance rule. Emergency copies can replace purchased copies which for any reason are not available for imminent performance, provided that the purchase copies are substituted later. For example, shortly before a school band is to play a concert the music teacher learns that six students have lost their music. The teacher is then entitled to make replacement copies for that performance. Later, the lost music would have to be found or purchased again.[3]

References to musical excerpts in books require that a publisher obtain permission for such a use by an author, since a few bars of a song can constitute the melodic line.

Apart from such specific limitations, fair use of music is beset with peril and should only be done with great caution, for the principles are clear enough but their application in specifics is not.[4]

It should also be noted that infringement cases in music, both religious and secular, occur frequently. Broadcast Music, Inc., sued Harvard University in 1978 for royalty fees because it, like some 1,000 other colleges it had contacted, had not signed licensing agreements for its music.[5] F. E. L. Publications, Ltd., won a decision over the Catholic Bishop of Chicago in 1984 for unlawful copying of its music by the Chicago Archdiocese in the amount of $3,000,000 in actual damages and $1,000,000 in punitive damages.[6]

Music — Usage Examples

Following are some questions and answers on fair use of music:

(1) A high school music teacher edits and simplifies some purchased sheet music for use with the choir. Is this o.k.? ***Yes.** Editing or simplifying purchased printed copies, as long as the work is not distorted or the lyrics (if there are any) are not altered or lyrics added where there were none.

(2) In evaluating student work, the professor makes a copy of the musical work performed by each student for his or her final grade that is then kept in a music library for subsequent student evaluation and comparison. ***Yes.** A copy may be made of a performance by students for evaluation or rehearsal purposes, and either the teacher or the institution may retain it.

(3) For a lesson on Renaissance music, a music teacher makes a copy of an aria of a song that is only available in a collection. ***Yes.** Making a single copy of a performable unit, such as a section, movement or aria, if the music is out of print or unavailable except in a larger work for research or class preparation, is permissible.

(4) For a unit on contemporary music, the music teacher makes a copy of Bob Seeger's "Night Moves" for the purpose of constructing a series of questions on the use of lyrics. ***Yes.** Copying a copyrighted sound recording for use in constructing aural exercises or examination is permissible.

(5) A combination of religious and popular inspirational music is sung by the school choir in an Easter service for an assembly. ***Yes.** Works performed in the course of a worship service or religious assembly are exempt.

(6) The school hires an acting troupe to present selections from *West Side Story* for an assembly. Neither the troupe nor the school

have paid royalties for this presentation. No admission is charged. *No. If an outside group of performers is paid to present an assembly, even a religious or charitable one, royalties have to be paid. It makes no difference if admission is charged or not. If outside performers are hired the performance is not exempt (Section 110[4]).

Music at the College and University Level

Royalties for noninstructional uses of copyrighted music, as well as instances when a performer is paid or admission is charged, require licensing fees to be paid to performing-rights agencies. The contracts can be blanket ones, covering several types of uses, or they can be negotiated on an individual basis.[7] These agencies are: The American Society of Composers, Authors, and Publishers (ASCAP), 1 Lincoln Plaza, New York NY 10023, 212-595-3050; Broadcast Music, Inc. (BMI), 320 W 57th St., New York NY 10019, 212-586-2000; and SESAC, Inc., formerly the Society of European Stage Authors and Composers, 10 Columbus Circle, New York NY 10019, 212-586-3450.

BMI, with over 1,000,000 titles, grants a blanket license for general uses of music, including noncommercial radio stations, according to the number of full-time students and full-time equivalent of part-time students. Commercial broadcasting stations affiliated with the college can also be covered by the license if they receive less than $10,000 a year from the sale of air time. Additional fees for concerts are based on the performer's fee and the seating capacity of the hall. ASCAP, with over 800,000 titles, also bases its fees on the number of full-time equivalent students. Additional fees for concerts vary according to seating capacity and top ticket price. SESAC, with over 140,000 titles, is based entirely on the number of students enrolled, and includes all nonbroadcast uses of music, with no additional per-concert fee. It also covers radio stations with transmitters of 20 watts or less. Higher wattage stations would receive a higher license rate.[8]

With the blanket license approach, performance of music at the halftime at football games, etc., is not subject to royalty payment unless the musicians are paid performers. Also covered are uses of music by student organizations, fraternities, sororities, etc.

Shortly after the new law came into effect, BMI sent letters to about 100 colleges asking them to stop playing music without obtaining a license. When Harvard, among others, refused to comply, the university was sued by BMI in 1979.[9] Subsequently, negotiations got under way for licensing agreements.

While there are some areas of usage that are questionable, the creation of the Copyright Royalty Commission will adjust royalty rates and distribute royalty fees over time (Sections 108–109).

5

Audiovisual Materials

Audiovisual works, as defined in Section 101, are works that:

consist of a series of related images ... shown by the use of ... projectors, viewers or electronic equipment, together with accompanying sounds, if any ...[1]

An audiovisual work could be filmstrips, slide sets, multi-media kits, motion pictures, or video games.[2] Motion pictures, whether in the form of 16 or 35 mm film or in the form of videotape, cassettes, or disks, are considered a class of audiovisual works.[3] This distinction is important, because since audiovisual works are not "nondramatic literary or musical works" (Section 110) their use in nonprofit educational institutions has become an area of controversy. Because of this clause, performance or display of audiovisual works may only be exempted: (1) for teaching and systematic instruction, (2) for home use (time shifting), and (3) with the copyright proprietor's permission.

Home-Use Taping and the School

The question of whether or not a teacher or librarian in a nonprofit educational institution could tape a program at home and then use it in teaching has yet to be answered. The *Sony* decision was a ruling on home use only.[4] Section 106 gives copyright owners the right to "display a work publicly." According to the *House Report* a work is displayed in public if it is in a "place open to the public or at any place where a substantial number of persons outside of a normal circle of a family

34

and its social acquaintances is gathered."[5] The *Report* states that performances at "clubs, lodges, factories, summer camps and schools" are to be considered "public."[6]

It is possible that, notwithstanding Section 106, fair use portions of audiovisual works could be used in nonprofit educational institutions. Fair use in this context would involve the use of a small segment of a program for teaching purposes. However, "librarying" of these segments or their use from term-to-term without obtaining permission could constitute copyright infringement.[7] These are aspects that will need clarification through the test of time.

Use in Nonprofit Educational Institutions

Use of audiovisuals in schools and other nonprofit endeavors must meet Section 110 criteria. Showings in fraternity and sorority houses, student recreation lounges, and in "video" theaters require licensing, either on a title-by-title or on a video blanket licensing program. Audiovisuals must be shown:

(1) *As part of "systematic instructional activities"*—in a teaching or learning environment of a classroom or library and not as a recreational or diversionary endeavor (Section 110[2][a]).

(2) *"Directly related ... to teaching"*—again, this is a prohibition against competition with movie houses or rental companies (Section 110[2][b]).

(3) *"In classroom or similar places"*—for example, a school or library could not rent a hall and show motion pictures not directly related to "systematic" teaching activities (110[2][i]).

(4) *"Without any purpose of direct or indirect commercial advantage"* (Section 110[4]).

(5) *"Without payment of any fee or other compensation ... [to] performers, promoters, or organizers"* (Section 110[4]).

Because of these stipulations, benefit performances where performers are hired would not qualify as an educational exemption, nor would recreational showings of motion pictures, whether on video or film, for employees, students, or guests of nonprofit institutions.

Performances would be exempt where the performers contributed their time. If admission was charged, "after deducting the reasonable costs of producing the performance" the proceeds must be "used exclusively for educational, religious, or charitable purposes and not for private financial gain."[8] In the event of an admission charge, the copyright owner must be given an opportunity to decide "whether and under what conditions the copyrighted work should be performed."[9] If the copyright owner objected in writing at least seven days before the performance, then that performance would be cancelled.[10]

Closed Circuit Viewing

For purposes of discussion, a work that is "displayed" would be a photograph or other artwork and Section 109 defines the ways in which the owner of a copy of a copyrighted work may use it.

Section 109 states that a copy may be displayed "to viewers present at the place where the copy is located." The *House Report* defines this phrase as:

> generally intended to refer to a situation in which viewers are present in the same physical surroundings as the copy, even though they cannot see the copy directly.

Obvious meanings for this situation would be a classroom, auditorium, or other such room. The *Report* specifically prohibits

> ... display of a visual image of a copyrighted work would be an infringement if the image were transmitted by any method (by closed or open circuit television, for example, or by computer system) from one place to members of the public located elsewhere.[11]

Because of the wording of the phrase, the question arises as to whether a work could be shown to classes in a school building or different rooms in a college building of a university via in-building closed circuit.

The same question arises with audiovisual works. A work that is "performed" would be an audiovisual, with or without accompanying sound, such as a motion picture, video, filmstrip, etc. Section 110 defines the ways in which the owner of a copy of a copyrighted work may use that type of medium. The *House Report* states that under Section 110, "Exemptions of Certain Performances and Displays":

"Face-to-face teaching activities" ... embrace instructional performances and displays that are not "transmitted." The concept does not require that the teacher and students be able to see each other, although it does require their simultaneous presence in the same general place. *Use of [this phrase] is intended to exclude broadcasting or other transmissions from an outside location into classrooms, whether radio or television and whether open or closed circuit.* However, as long as the instructor and pupils are in the same building or general area, the exemption would extend to the use of devices for amplifying or reproducing sound and for projecting visual images.[12]

As in the case of displayed works, while closed circuit use is specifically prohibited, the meaning of the language is still unclear. Using closed circuit to display or perform a work campus-wide in a college or other large institution with multiple buildings or to transmit to colleges, as in a university setting, would probably be an infringement of copyright. Controversy continues; however, since closed circuit use is specifically prohibited, the balance of current opinion seems to be that transmission to classrooms is prohibited, unless with the permission of the copyright owner.

To avoid possible legal entanglement, some districts and institutions have written request forms for closed circuit viewing while others either call the producer or request closed circuit permission when purchasing the audiovisual.

The Off-Air Taping Guidelines

Called the "Guidelines for Off-Air Recording of Broadcast Programming for Educational Purposes," they represent the first concrete agreement on off-air taping.[13] Now, commercial broadcast programs, including those simultaneously broadcast on cable, PBS programs cleared for taping, and certain cable programs can be taped. However, many educational media producers do not want any part of their work reproduced because their materials are designed for education.[14] In addition, categories of programs which cannot be taped are those available for purchase and rental and those on subscription television, which requires a user fee.

Negotiations did not begin formally until 1979, when the

Committee to Negotiate Off-Air Videotaping Guidelines was appointed, composed of education organizations, copyright proprietors, and creative guilds and unions. In the meantime, educators adopted versions of the PBS seven-day standard for programs cleared for taping until guidelines could be established.[15]

There can be little doubt that some of the impetus for these guidelines came from a suit brought against the Board of Cooperative Educational Services (BOCES) of Erie County, New York, by three film companies — Encyclopaedia Britannica, Learning Corporation of America, and Time-Life Films in 1978. Off-air taping had been done by BOCES over several years. In the 1976–77 school year alone BOCES duplicated approximately 10,000 tapes of copyrighted motion pictures. It maintained videotape equipment worth a half million dollars and employed five to eight people. Educational services were provided to over 100 public schools. No records were maintained of how many times each videotape was viewed or its disposition after use.[16]

The court ordered that BOCES cease taping the companies' educational films off the airwaves and obtain proper licenses for such use that were available. Other films which had been videotaped and incorporated into the curricula were allowed to be distributed as long as a plan was implemented to monitor the use of the tapes and require their return and erasure within a specified time period.

In keeping with this decision, the guidelines made it clear that duplication of programs available through licensing, inadequate record keeping and disposal of tapes after use add up to infringement. "Intentional substitution" of a program taped off-air to avoid rental is not only a cause for a lawsuit, but it is also unethical. Quite often the licensing fee for use of a program is a necessary way of figuring the profit to be made in its production.[17]

The Provisions of the Guidelines

The period during which a program may be shown is ten days. During that time a program may be shown once "in the course of relevant teaching activities," and then repeated once only for reinforcement purposes. No definition is provided for what constitutes "the course of relevant teaching activities," whether it includes a class for which a teacher has more than one section or not. However, until the guidelines have been tested and made more clear, it seems reasonable to assume that a teacher who instructs more than one section of a class, such as three sections of English 101, would be in keeping with the guidelines if a tape was shown to those sections, as long as proper use records were kept.

After the initial ten-day period, the instructor has 35 more days in which to review the tape. This 45-day holding period does not include weekends, holidays, vacations, examination periods, or other scheduled interruptions. In effect, the holding period lasts around two months. At the end of that period the tape must be erased or destroyed immediately.

A "limited number" of copies may be made to meet the "legitimate needs" of requesting teachers, but each request must be initiated by the teacher. This does not prevent the media specialist from alerting faculty of programs that might be beneficial. Regardless of the number of times a program is broadcast, it can only be taped once for that teacher.

"Limited number" is a vague term. Perhaps after the guidelines have been in use in the schools and certain other unforeseen technological developments occur this term might be better defined. In the meantime, the media specialist and teacher should make sure that a tape is requested for "legitimate needs" which can be defined as being part of systematic instructional activities, directly related to teaching content, and intended to be shown in the classroom. Copies should not be made indiscriminately (Section 110).[18]

Other provisions are:

(1) Tapes can only be used in "classrooms and similar places of instruction" for nonprofit educational institutions. Uses outside the classroom during the ten-day showing or the 35-day holding periods would require authorization. Such uses would include student exhibition during the holding period, use in a library, showing for parent-teacher and student groups, etc.

(2) A tape may be used only "within a single building, cluster, or campus, as well as in the home of students receiving formalized home instruction." Loaning of tapes, or distribution of tapes off-campus, is prohibited.[19]

(3) While the program does not have to be shown in its entirety, it cannot be altered from the original content, or physically or electronically merged to constitute a compilation or anthology.

(4) Regardless of the number of times a program is broadcast, it can only be taped once for that teacher.

(5) All copies of a program must include the notice of copyright on the broadcast program as recorded.

(6) Lastly, institutions are expected "to establish appropriate control procedures" to ensure that the guidelines are followed. This could be interpreted to mean that adequate record keeping of the name of the requester, the date it was taped, the name of the program, and the class it was used for is maintained. A mechanism to prevent retaping or reshowing a tape should be initiated, whether it is a check-out system or some other device, to ensure that the guidelines are followed.

While there are some questions that will naturally arise as the guidelines are used and tested, they seem to be a reasonable solution for the off-air quandary that education has been in for the last several years.[20]

Satellite Off-Air Taping

Schools and colleges are beginning to purchase satellite dishes for increased educational benefit to students. Use of satellite dishes for this purpose raises questions as to the legality of taping programs via satellite. The answers, however, are not clear-cut. Legal opinion is divided on the permissibility of this practice as programmers, dish makers, and owners continue to negotiate.[21]

It currently appears that regular broadcast programming, as is seen on the major broadcast stations such as NBC, ABC, CBS, and programs cleared for taping through PBS which are simultaneously rebroadcast, is permissible under the "Guidelines for Off-Air Recording of Broadcast Programming for Educational Purposes" (see Appendix C). Other programming, from such programmers as "The Disney Channel," "The Discovery Channel," etc., requires licenses of varying amounts.

It is these other programmers (not the major broadcasters such as ABC) that are not subject to copyright law, as currently written. This programming is governed by the Communications Act of 1934 (488 Stat. 1064), as amended (P.L. 98–549, Cable Communications Policy Act of 1984), to include satellite programming. This act does not employ the concept of "fair use" and therefore all use is subject to licensing.

Just how the concept of satellite taping in the school will be resolved will depend on future usage trends and the steps that both educators and programmers will take on their own behalfs to insure equitable use.

Teacher Local Video Rental

Because of the ease and convenience of renting videos from local retail outlets, teachers are beginning to rent videos for classroom use. While most uses for this purpose are legally permissible, some are not.

One of the conditions of Section 102 is that motion picture and video exhibition must be a part of "systematic instructional activities." This means that any showing of a video for purely entertainment purposes would be an infringement. For example, showing a video of *Romeo and Juliet* in an English class during a unit on Shakespeare would be permissible. Showing *Back to the Future* or other such entertainment features on a dull Friday afternoon without an instructional rationale would not. *House Report 94-1476* states:

> The "teaching activities" exempted by the clause encompass systematic instruction of a very wide variety of subjects, but they do not include performances or displays, whatever their cultural value or intellectual appeal, that are given for the recreation or entertainment of any part of their audience.

A display of a rented video for instructional purposes would include a library, gym, auditorium, or workshop, provided it is used as a classroom.[22] (See also the School Libraries section of Chapter 10, and Use in Nonprofit Educational Institutions section on pages 35–36 above).

Format Changes

In changing formats of audiovisual materials, such as from filmstrip to slide or record to cassette, apart from copyright, an important question is whether or not the use is intended to increase the wear of the original materials. If so, such an act would be unfair use, unless permission was obtained.

In some instances, changing formats is necessitated by obsolete equipment or when part of an audiovisual package is unusable (such as the cassette in a slide/tape kit) and the producer is not making them any more, is out of business, or will not respond to queries. In cases such as these such a change really does no harm to the author's market.

In many instances, 16mm films, videocassettes, filmstrips and audiocassette tapes may be exchanged for a new one, purchased at a discount, depending on the producer. An instructor who regularly makes copies of purchased tapes, slides, etc., is performing illegal acts, whether he or she is sued or not. A district education center serving 10,000 students at six schools that makes multiple copies for its schools without proper clearance would be infringing. [23]

As with print materials, viewing a use in the eyes of the reasonable copyright owner should cover the great majority of uses.

The Video Future and Copyright

Newer areas of technology such as teletext and videotext, interactive video, and hardware changes, such as from videocassette to disk and compact disk, will affect future use of copyrighted materials.

Teletext-written material and graphics shown on a television screen, while increasingly used in industry, is a new development in education, and there are teletext projects in different parts of the country. While some of the projects are free to subscriber schools, in the future the service will probably require a fee from user schools. The projected use of teletext would require the use of a decoder placed inside a television set to receive the program, in much the way that UHF is a standard part of television sets today.

It is envisioned that each station would carry its own version of a teletext "magazine." It is conceivable, in the near future, that some stations would carry a subscription service, and would scramble the signals except to those sets with special decoders. These services would be copyrighted, and would be as much off-limits to copying as subscription television is to off-air taping for educational uses. The development of this type of service, along with the use of hard copy printers for the teletext magazine, should see more interesting developments in the area of copyright. Some possible uses for the teletext service would be special interest programs or educational programs on different subjects.

Interactive video—the combination of computer and videotape or cassette for programmed instruction—is being marketed to industry and medicine, but the development of interactive video programs commercially for education is rising. In-house production of both the tape and the program is time-consuming, difficult, and expensive, but newer equipment is making interactive systems more attractive. Adaptation of a commercially-produced program to interactive video does require authorization. Most programs being done now are original because of the special needs of this medium. A marked increase in use of interactive video in schools would be needed before the need arises to develop rules of usage.

The videodisk and compact disk, which are superior to the videotape in terms of visual capability and program capacity, are progressing rapidly. However, current technology, which requires the additional costs of mastering the disk and then having it reproduced, is still in the development stages.

Format changes, such as from videotape to videodisk, will also affect the use of copyrighted materials in the future, and it is expected that such changes would require permission from the publisher. The introduction of videodisks, which currently cannot be used to copy programs, could be effective in reducing copying. A machine could be introduced in the future, however, that could copy a disk inexpensively.

Audiovisual Materials—Usage Examples

The following are some examples of fair use of audiovisuals.

(1) An instructor makes small excerpts on cassette audiotapes for use in demonstrating various music styles. ***Yes.** Small excerpts for use in teaching and scholarship is fair use.

(2) A teacher makes a videotape for television class and illustrates the talk with small clips from current television shows to illustrate theme and content. ***Yes.** Small clips for instructional purposes are exempt and considered fair use.

(3) For a film technique class, the instructor rents a film for class use and makes four slides to illustrate point-of-view in directing. ***Yes.** Making a small number of slides for classroom use is fair use.

(4) Only the audio portion of a television documentary is taped from a program on PBS and is kept permanently by the teacher for classroom use. *****The off-air taping or audio taping of a television

program for a one-time classroom use is permissible under the off-air taping guidelines. However, a tape **must be erased** no later than 45 days after taping. It cannot be kept without permission or rental.[24] It is possible that permission would be granted for audio only. Retaining a small portion of the documentary is fair use.

(5) A teacher makes a copy of a program on commercial television at home and uses the program at school for instructional purposes. *It is **unclear** how the courts would view such a use. The Supreme Court rules only in the *Sony* case on in-home noncommercial copying for in-home use only. It was a narrow decision that noted that other uses, such as the above-mentioned, were not included. While there is some support for such a use if it was spontaneous, it would depend on the individual circumstances, such as if the tape was subsequently kept in the school library, if the tape was used once or many times, if such taping was done systematically, etc.

(6) A teacher would like to show a rented video of *Star Wars* on the last day of school. Is this permissible? *No, if it is a locally rented video shown solely for entertainment purposes. Only uses which are part of "systematic instructional activities" are permissible. Because this video would likely be presented for entertainment, the classroom exception would not apply. However, if the video were rented through a standard film and video catalog for a fee, such a use would be permissible.

Examples of Change of Format

(1) A school district buys one copy of a 16mm film and makes five tapes for use in its schools. *No. Making copies of a film without license or agreement is infringement.

(2) A media department regularly converts phonograph records into audiocassettes for individual teachers. *No. Conversion of records on a regular basis without license or permission is illegal.

(3) A media center has six 1″ videotapes that are 15 years old. The videotape machine that was used is no longer in working condition and buying a new one is impractical since ¾″ formats are now being used exclusively by the center. The librarian tried to contact the producer but found that the company was out of business. Can the 1″ tapes be converted to ¾″ tapes? *Yes. Under most circumstances, copying a tape still protected by copyright would be an infringement. However, if the librarian tried to contact the producer then conversion could not harm

sales. All reasonable means should be exhausted before copying a copy-righted tape. The librarian is obligated to make all reasonable attempts to contact the producer for permission. Permission can be granted or a reduced price for a tape in a new format can be given or it can be required that a new tape must be purchased. It depends on the producer.

(4) An art instructor needs 50 slides for an art history class. Because they are unavailable for purchase, he requests that they be copied from an art book. *No. The large number of slides and the like-lihood that they will be used from term to term makes this an illegal use. Permission should be requested.

(5) For a class in physiology, the instructor purchases a set of slides and requests that five duplicate sets be made from it for use in lab sessions. *No. If five sets of slides are needed then five sets of slides should be purchased.

(6) An instructor makes a copy of a 1903 copyrighted silent film for classroom use. *Yes. A film copyrighted in 1903 is in the public domain if it was copyrighted by a company (75 year term). A film copyrighted by an individual has the term of the life of the author plus 50 years, but these are relatively rare.

6
Computer Software

Copyright is the most common protection for programs used by the general public.[1] While there are other forms of protection commonly used by producers, such as trade secret and "unfair competition" provisions, patent protection has not been extended to microcomputer programs as yet. The need for copyright protection of computer programs has grown in proportion to three related trends. Size and expense of computers dropped tremendously. At the same time, programs became more frequently written for the general public for use in the home, office, and school.[2]

In addition to copyright law, there are other methods of protecting a program from being copied, such as special coding. These methods of protection are as ingenious and varied as the producers. Minnesota Education Computing Consortium (MECC) backup disks have a special counter which allows only a certain number of copies to be made, for example. Most programs will have special bugs put in the program that will blank the screen, self-destruct, or make it very difficult to copy the entire program. The use of other formats, such as cartridges which cannot be copied, will alter copying.

Copyright protection was available as early as 1964, when the U.S. Copyright Office began issuing certification of registration for copyright of computer programs and in that year programs were first mentioned in a revision bill.[3] Because experts were not sure which direction the protection of computer programs should take, Congress handed the question of copyright protection over to the National Commission on New Technological Uses (CONTU) to study the matter and make recommendations in 1978. The *House Report* on Section 117 of the 1978 Copyright Act stated that Congress would extend protection

46

to computer programs as a new kind of literary work, and that CONTU would study the matter and make recommendations at a later date.[4]

On the recommendations of CONTU, the Act was amended December 12, 1980.[5] Two changes were made: computer programs were specifically defined as literary works (Section 101), and Section 117 was rewritten to allow the owner of a program to make or authorize the making of a copy or adaptation provided that it is an essential step in the use of the program and that it is for archival purposes only and would be destroyed if the original was sold or given away.

As with other literary works under the new copyright law, computer programs are eligible for copyright protection as soon as they are written or recorded in a medium of expression, such as on a tape, disk, or chip.[6] However, registration is necessary, in most cases, before an action for copyright infringement may be instituted.[7] Works such as computer programs, music, and other hotly contested copyright works should be filed as quickly as possible. Not only is the program on the tape or disk protected, but accompanying manuals and lesson guides are eligible for copyright protection, as well.

The Rights of the Producer

The exclusive rights of the producer of the program are:

(1) reproduction of copies (excluding fair use portions and archival copies);
(2) production of derivative works (such as machine-specific versions);
(3) distribution of copies for sale or leasing;
(4) performance of the work publicly, if audiovisual (such as a video game);
(5) display of a work, if graphic, publicly.

A computer program is different than the other media because in some ways it is like film and in others it is like print. It includes manuals, and the manuals and the program can be put on a printout. As with film, merely running a program without paying for it can be an infringement. As with books, making copies of the manuals or documentation without permission or purchase is also an infringement. While in practice some producers allow more than one copy to be made, the archival copy is the only copy that may be made apart from such agreements.[8] A copy made for the user's archival purposes is legally permissible, unless the use of copies has been agreed upon when the program was purchased through the license or purchase agreement.[9]

The lease or purchase of a program for a school or district will stipulate how the program can be used and under what conditions it can be copied. Depending on the circumstances of the contract, copying could be allowed for a higher fee under a multiple copy license.

The Rights of the User

The individual or institution that purchases a program also has certain rights:

(1) To make one or more copies for archival purposes to guard against destruction or damage through mechanical failure.
(2) To make the necessary adaptations in order to use the program correctly.
(3) To add features to the program so long as it is not sold or given away without the author's permission.

Programs in the public domain can be adapted, compiled, abridged, or translated into another language. If the new work is sufficiently original, the copyright applies only to the new adaptation, compilation, etc.[10]

Database Downloading

Automated databases are a new class of copyrightable works, and have generally been considered copyrightable as compilations.[11] Databases are defined in the *House Report* as "literary works."[12] Section 101 defines a compilation as:

formed by the collection and assembling of pre-existing materials or of data that are selected, coordinated, or arranged in such a way that the resulting work as a whole constitutes an original work of authorship.

"Downloading" involves the transmission of data from a remote or host computer to the user's on-site storage device for later searching, manipulation, or storage.[13] With the increased use of microcomputers for online searching, decreasing costs of database services, and increased sophistication of programs which could manipulate the data once downloaded, downloading is becoming easier.[14] Network speeds are also increasing; 1200- to 2400- are currently available and distribution of a 9600-baud modem (though not currently compatible with most database vendors and communications programs) has begun. Downloading becomes more attractive on a financial basis in which connect-time to the vendor is the basis for the fee.[15]

Downloading is difficult to detect under the present connect-time rate system. In addition, vendor activity reports are generally insufficient to detect such activity. They indicate, in most cases, the name of the user, the number of connect hours used, and the number of offline and online prints. It would be possible to surmise that a search which resulted in a large number of hits (records) in a very short connect time would indicate downloading, yet, a system for detecting downloading has yet to be devised.[16]

While many database producers sell their database as a spinoff from the hard-copy product, receiving 80 percent turnover from the printed product, subscriptions are declining and it is conjectured that "online products are considered to be future replacements for the printed products."[17] Proposed remedies for this problem are nontransaction pricing schemes, changes in delivery formats, and controlled amounts of downloading in licensing agreements.[18]

Infringement

Courts have found that databases are copyrightable whether they consist of all copyrighted material or of all or predominantly public domain material, because of the original compilation of elements.[19] Transfer to an in-house computer is considered to be making copy.[20] Unauthorized substantial downloading from a commercial vendor is considered infringement, whether of public domain or copyrighted material, as is the use of special database access routines to bypass royalties or unauthorized baud rates to download data.[21]

The issue of what constitutes copyright infringement in other instances has many unanswered aspects. The scope and degree of copyright protection has yet to be defined, as does the doctrinal basis — editorial selection, arrangement of data, and or industriousness.[22] Scanning a copyrighted database without proper payment or authorization could be an infringement, as could unauthorized downloading of a search of a program.[23]

Database vendors and producers, in an effort to deal with what promises to be much greater downloading, are beginning to examine the type of use to be made of the data rather than just the act of downloading. INSPEC (a database vendor) has identified three general classes of downloading:

(1) *Temporary storage* — storage for a limited time for search purposes and destruction of the records afterward.

(2) *Long-term storage and reuse at the downloading site* — use within an organization for up to a year or more at the downloading site with reuse of downloaded records for various purposes.

(3) *Other uses* — such as multiple copying of data, specialized databases, and information bulletins reviews.[24]

Temporary storage. The fairness of using records downloaded for delayed search purposes and then discarded immediately would depend on the circumstances of the use. Copying one record would be considered fair use and is clearly not grounds for infringement.[25] Copying a substantial portion of a database would be considered infringement.[26] However, the line where fair use ends and infringement begins has yet to be drawn. The fact that downloading license agreements typically allow temporary storage at no extra charge indicates the reluctance of database vendors to pursue an infringement action in what might be found to be a limited use.[27]

The fairness of *long-term storage* in a user's own organization would also depend on the circumstances of the case. The amount downloaded, the length of storage time, its use within the organization or elsewhere, its use at the downloading site or at a place other than at the downloading site, as well as any commercial use of downloaded records, for example, would determine infringement.

For this reason, downloading agreements, from such database vendors as INSPEC, DIALOG, BIOSIS, and others, specify their terms and conditions for this type of storage. Frequently, the conditions are that such storage is within the terms of the agreement, provided that it is used only within the organization and that there is no intent for resale or transfer to other than the downloading site.

Other uses: downloading substantial portions of a database for commercial use or resale, such as for multiple copying of data, information bulletins, specialized databases, etc., with the intent of resale or without authorization from the vendor is infringement.[28] Database infringement cases to date have involved the reproduction of 80 percent to 100 percent of a program. What amount, as well as other factors to be considered in infringement, will require further judicial interpretation.

Fair Use

Judicial doctrine increasingly supports the principle that:

copyright protection for compilations of factual material cannot be reconciled with the general principles of the copyright laws ... such works should be conducive to fair use. Authors of compilations, therefore, must be held to grant broader license for subsequent use than persons whose work is truly creative.[29]

Legal opinion generally agrees that databases and compilations allow fair use to a greater degree than other literary works.[30] Fair use is very limited where the intent is for commercial use.[31] Downloading under authorized means (such as under a downloading license agreement, for example) of small portions of databases to be temporarily retained for the purposes of teaching, research, scholarship, or criticism is fair use. Downloading to prepare a concordance of a work or to perform a syntactical analysis of a work, with the records discarded after use, would be considered fair.[32] However, keeping archival copies of downloaded works, absent a downloading license agreement, would require the copyright owner's permission.[33] Downloading a small portion of a database into temporary storage for a delayed search for scholarly or nonprofit purposes (without intent for resale), after which the records were immediately discarded, could be considered fair use.[34]

Fair use of databases would be subject to the four fair use criteria:

(1) the purpose and character of the use, whether material is downloaded for profit or nonprofit use. In cases of profit use, fair use is greatly reduced.

(2) Nature of the copyrighted work, whether from a commercial vendor or from a nonprofit or in-house database.

(3) The amount and substantiality of the material used.

(4) The effect of the use upon the potential market. Uses that directly or potentially deprive the producer of database sales can be cause for infringement.

Implications for the Future

Downloading of software via such commercial database vendors as The Source or CompuServe has recently become possible. Plans are underway for other commercial vendors to make downloading of software available on a wider scale. The emergence of new forms of software sales will create new problems of theft of software via electronic means.

A bill was introduced in 1984 which would strengthen the laws against computer programs and database piracy and counterfeiting by increasing the maximum penalties to five years' imprisonment and or a fine of $250,000. This bill would impose the same penalties now applicable to record, tape, and film piracy, and label counterfeiting.[35] It is likely that statutory as well as judicial clarification is on the horizon.

Computer Software — Usage Examples

(1) I have some programs that can be multiply booted (loaded into more than one machine). Is it legal to do this? *No, it isn't, unless you have a site license or multiple copy license from the publisher. In practice, some programs can be used this way, such as word processing and database management programs. However, multiple booting of a program is considered to be much the same as making pirated copies. Two companies were successfully sued for just such practices. While some producers, such as Sunburst, will allow more than one machine to be booted with some of their programs, this is a decision that only the producer can make. The MECC programs are very good for multiple booting purposes, since a site license is relatively inexpensive. If multiple loading is a useful strategy, public domain software can be helpful. Public domain programs have no copyright and legally may be loaded multiply from a single disk. Two sources of public domain software are the Computer Learning Center, POB 111086, Tacoma WA

98499; and Softswap, San Mateo County Office of Education, 333 Main Street, Redwood City CA 94063.

(2) What is the difference between programs that have been purchased outright and those that have been leased? *If a program is leased (and this is a growing trend, just as with videocassettes), then it is subject to certain use restrictions, just as if a videocassette or film were leased or rented. The license itself will explain these terms. The principle of the license is that unless it is specifically allowed it should not be done.

A program purchased outright, which usually costs much more than a leased program and is custom made, has different terms. In such cases, there are no restrictions on how many copies may be made, so multiple copies are fair, as long as they are not given or sold to others. Just as with leased software, the purchaser does not have the right to make a copy and distribute it.[36]

(3) I purchased a program that is copy protected, and a backup was not supplied. May I use a "nibble copier" or "locksmith" program to make a back-up? *The law states that the purchaser of a program may make or authorize the making of an archival copy to guard against human or mechanical damage. The language of the law, however, is unclear as to who is responsible for supplying the back-up—the producer or the purchaser. If the disk is not copy protected, meaning it was designed so copies cannot be made through normal copying procedures, then it is your legal right to make one archival copy. The purpose of an archival copy is only to keep one in an archival file. A back-up copy is not to be used as a *second* copy of the original; it is only to be used in the event of damage to the original.

If the disk is copy protected, then the producer should supply a back-up at a reasonable price. Although most producers are beginning to supply back-ups at a reasonable price, many still do not. Software publishers have taken companies to court over illegal copying.[37] However, no software publisher has taken a school to court over alleged illegal copying, nor has any school taken a producer to court over the right to a back-up—yet.

(4) Should I request an archival copy (back-up) when purchasing school software? *Yes. These magnetic media are fragile. Power surges, human misuse, disk drive problems, etc., can ruin a disk. An archival copy can be used in place of the original until a new disk is received. Many producers will send a replacement disk for a small fee if the original is returned.

Several producers believe that backups are used by school districts as second copies of the original. This is not what the law intended. P.L. 96–517 (the computer amendment) states that the purchaser of a program may make an archival copy or authorize one to be made to guard against human or mechanical damage. Order from producers that supply a backup at reasonable price and notify those that do not. Sunburst, Educational Activities, Hartley, and others will usually supply one and a growing number of directories, such as *TESS–The Educational Software Selector Software Reports* and others, include this information. The International Council for Computers in Education (ICCE) has been very vocal about the need for backups and as a result the number of producers supplying backups has increased.

7

Contributions, Articles, Registration

Contributions to Collective Works

Section 201d discusses "contributions to collective works" in this way:

> Copyright in each separate contribution to a collective work is distinct from copyright in the collective work as a whole, and rests initially in the author of the contribution. *In the absence of an express transfer of the copyright or of any rights under it, the owner of copyright in the collective work is presumed to have acquired only the privilege of reproducing and distributing the contribution as a part of that collective work, and any later collective work in that series.*

According to the *House Report*, a collective work is defined as a periodical issue, anthology, or encyclopedia, in which a number of contributions, each separate, independent and pre-existing, are assembled into one whole.[1] The result, if originally combined, is considered a collective work. Because of this change in the law, a publisher can copyright individual issues of a periodical as "collective works"—that is, copyright the collection, and not need to require that an author surrender copyright of the individual piece. Two separate copyrights can exist.

Many copyright agreements routinely used for author acceptance of the publication of a work ask assignment of the author's copyright as well. There is no longer any need for such as assignment, since the prerequisite of publication for copyright protection has been abolished and each issue of a periodical or other such collective work may be copyrighted separately.

Assigning copyright for a work to a publisher or producer may be of little concern to an author in certain instances, and even be useful and convenient when no further recognition or remuneration is anticipated. However, if the author wishes to maintain control over the published work for reprint or other purposes, it is advisable that the author retain the original copyright and remind the journal that retention of the individual copyright in no way abrogates the right of the publisher to copyright the collective work. Many journals are either unaware of the difference, or find it better to request the individual copyright, as well.

Should the author wish to retain individual copyright, then the owner of the collective copyright (a journal, for example) is presumed to have acquired only the privilege of reproducing and distributing the contribution as a part of its collective work. Depending on the nature of the contract, the publisher could then be given permission to reprint the article in a later version of work, but the publisher would not have the right to grant a reprint of the article in a work by another publisher (such as another journal or in a book by another publisher).[2] In instances where the author wishes to retain copyright of the individual article, it is often advised that the author make it a requirement in writing that the author retains copyright of the work. The article will then bear a separate notice of copyright, and this notice is sufficient to indicate that the author retained copyright of the work.[3]

Among the rights that the collective work publisher does not have if the copyright is retained are (1) to distribute reprints of the article, (2) to license translation rights, (3) to authorize photocopying beyond fair use and library exemptions, (4) to produce microform editions, and (5) to use or permit use of the article in a computerized database.[4]

Scholarly Journal Reprints/Requests

In the case of reprints, if the journal retains copyright, and there is no clause in the standard contract for reprint notification, then the journal quite possibly would not notify the author of reprint requests. In sending back a standard journal contract, one option would be to add a sentence stating that the author wishes notification in case of reprints. A better option would be to examine the contract to see if there is a clause for notification of reprints. If there isn't, it would be better for the author to retain copyright. In most cases, retention of copyright would not be a hindrance to the publication of the author's material in a journal.

Should another writer take the author's work and put it into his or her own work without notification, then the copyright owner takes legal action, if desired. Should the author have signed his or her copyright over to a journal, the journal or publisher has the legal right to pursue the matter, or not to. The author may wish to notify the journal from which the material was taken and then consult an attorney, as well.

Registration

For one who is contemplating the "poor man's" copyright (via registered mail—see page 14), there are inducements to registration. In general, a work must be registered before a suit for copyright infringement can be filed.[5]

Unless a work had been registered before a particular act of infringement occurred, the copyright owner cannot recover statutory damages and attorney's fees for an infringement. However, there is a three-month grace period beginning on the date of publication and if an infringement occurs during that three month period and if registration is made before the end of the three months, the copyright owner is still eligible for statutory damages and attorney's fees.[6]

In addition to the increased validity of the copyright owner's claim of copyright in an infringement action, works registered before or within five years after publication also receive certain other practical advantages, such as in licensing, royalty collection, transfer, etc.[7]

8

Permissions

Because of the nature of fair use, there will be times when the line between "fair" and "unfair" will be unclear. In those situations, the questions to be asked are: Is the material important? Is the time needed to get permission reasonable? Could the use bring about a lawsuit?

If the answer is "yes" to one or more of these questions, then obtaining permission would be in the best interest of all concerned. An efficient policy will save time, trouble and duplicated effort.

Even with the "broad insulation" intended for the educator and nonprofit user by the new "innocent infringer" provision, there will be times when an infringement case could be raised.[1] If one is brought up there are several possible results:

(1) The user could win and pay nothing.
(2) The user could win and pay court costs and attorney's fees.
(3) The user could lose, pay a $100 fine, court costs and attorney's fees.
(4) The user could lose, pay a $100 fine, court costs, and attorney's fees for both parties.
(5) The user could pay up to $50,000 fine for one or more violations in criminal infringement, court costs, attorney's fees for him or herself, and possibly for the other party.[2]

As is evident, even if the instructor or the institution were innocent, he or she and it *could* pay.

Once it has been decided to seek permission, there are procedures that can simplify the process. Certain types of permissions are generally granted without a fee. They are:

(1) Requests for quotations from scholarly books where the use may be more extensive than what is normally considered fair.
(2) Transcripts for the blind.
(3) Requests for reproduction of portions of material to be used one time, in an experimental situation or in a curriculum development program.
(4) Requests for selections of a book or its illustrations for reviews or articles concerning the book.[3]

Douglas (audiovisuals) and Mucklow (print) found variations in the granting of permissions and the fees for usage.[4] Situations can be unique. Douglas gave examples of permissions from her own experience. One publisher allowed the making of 500 copies of a short story for a $12 fee and a credit line. Another publisher allowed reproduction of a series of tests (prohibited from fair use under the guidelines). The last publisher would not grant permission because inexpensive reprints (50¢ each) were available. Mucklow found that text and illustrations generally did not require a fee for educational use. Photographs and poems ran from no charge to $50 each.

The responses vary according to the publisher or author, the circumstances of the use, and the type of material being reproduced.

Permissions and the Publisher

Unless the author retains copyright, it is the publisher and not the author who answers permissions request. Unpublished materials would, of course, be directed to the person who wrote it. Publishers examine requests carefully. The more exact the information in the request the more efficiently the permission is handled. The American Association of Publishers (AAP) and the Authors League (AL) say in their pamphlet on uses and permissions that "one of the most frequent reasons cited by permissions departments for delays in answering request of this nature is incomplete or inaccurate information contained in the request."[5]

Granting a request involves a check on the status of copyright, obtaining and determining exactly what the material is for which the permission is requested (it could be in the warehouse), and calculating and assigning royalty fees to the author, if they are needed.

There are four questions a publisher must answer to fulfill a request:

(1) Is the permission consistent with any agreement with the author?

(2) Is the material used the author's own, or is it something for which he or she had (or has) to get permission?

(3) What is the amount requested and how will it be used?

(4) Should there be quantitative limits (number of copies), time limits (one-time or repeated usage), or geographic limits (institutional or off-campus)?

The Request Format for Print Materials

The address and phone number of the publisher, if not on the work, can be obtained from *Literary Market Place* or *Publishers' Trade List Annual* for books, *Writer's Market* for books and periodicals, *Computer Books and Serials in Print* for computer-oriented materials, and *Ulrich's International Periodicals Directory*. An initial phone call can facilitate the request greatly; discussing in advance the intended use, charges, and the information needed by the publisher to grant the request can save time. In a few cases, a single phone call will do, as a fee may not be required.

If a fee is likely, then a follow-up letter is necessary. It should name the contact and the date the call was made. Form letters have mixed success. In some large institutions where a usage is questionable, but not far from a clearly fair use, a form letter might be all that is necessary. But if a use is important, or if it is clearly more than fair use, the request should warrant an individually typed letter.

The format should include:

(1) The title, author, editor, or compiler, and the edition used.

(2) The exact amount of material to be used, page numbers, and a photocopy of the material requested, if possible.

(3) A reference to the contact person by name in the letter if the initial contact was made by phone.

(4) The nature of the use, including how many times the material will be used, whether on- or off-campus, and whether in classrooms or in promotional mailings, etc.

(5) The number of copies to be made.

(6) How the material will be reproduced (ditto, off-set, photocopy, etc.).

Sample Print Permissions Letter

January 25, 1987

Permissions Department
School Book Company
Wichita KS 67217

Dear Director:

I would like permission for one of our instructors, Deta Baker, to duplicate the following for classroom use next semester (beginning September, 1987):

Author:	Linda Halvin
Title:	*Studies in Modern Sociology*, 3rd ed., 1979 (out of print).
Copyright:	1975, 1979.
Material to be duplicated:	pages 23–33 of Chapter 2 — "Quantitative Methods" (photocopies enclosed).
Number of copies:	33
Form of distribution:	supplied to students gratis for classroom use in fall semester only.
Type of reprint:	photocopy

The page above will be used as a supplementary reading for the class "Advanced quantitative methods in sociological research."

Enclosed is a self-addressed, stamped envelope.

Sincerely,

June Sanger, Director
Rossmore Media Center
Maricopa Community Center
Los Angeles CA 90020

The AAP and AL also suggest that one request all permissions for specific projects at the same time, and that one not ask for blanket permission — which cannot, in most cases, be granted.[6]

The Request Format for Videos

The address and phone number of the producer, if not known, can be obtained from *How to Acquire Legal Copies of Video Programs*, or the *Video Source Book*, or the *NICEM Index to Educational Video-tapes*. If possible, an initial phone call is recommended, as programs are often negotiable, depending on the intended use.

In requesting to make a videotape copy or in requesting to retain a copy made according to the "Off-Air Taping Guidelines," much the same information should be requested as for print materials. The format should include:

(1) Title.
(2) Type of reproduction (½", ¾").
(3) If only a portion of the tape is required, then name section and minutes of portion.
(4) Number of copies.
(5) Nature of use, specific class and class size, if possible, and nature of transmission, whether closed circuit (CCTV) or instructional fixed service (ITFS).
(6) If initial contact was made by phone, refer to contact name in letter.

Microcomputer Software License Requests

While standard packages can be acquired (5 packs, 10 packs) of certain software, normally database, word processing, and spreadsheet applications and site licenses for large groups (often based on annual daily attendance–ADA formulas) must be negotiated individually. This can be based on one or more programs that the producer or distributor may have. For example, three programs could be negotiated for as a package, just as it could be done for one. If possible, it is best to negotiate based on class size rather than the size of the school.

In preparing to request licensing for software, various directories providing names, addresses, and phone numbers can be used. However, not all companies publish information on special volume discounts or on-site licensing. This information can often only be obtained by a phone call, if possible, or a letter. *Classroom Computer Learning* publishes an annual directory, and software reviewing tools such as *TESS* (The Educational Software Selector) available from EPIE (Educational Products and Information Exchange), *Software Reports, Software Reviews on File, Digest of Software Reviews* etc., may be used. Acquiring microcomputer software licensing (with the notable exception of MECC software) is based on the variables of school district, or consortium size, number of microcomputers, and the proclivity of the individual producer or distributor. At present, there seems to be much variation.

Permissions Policies

In requesting permission, whether for royalty purposes or not, there are five steps to be followed:

(1) Call or mail the request.
(2) If initial contact was made by phone, refer to the contact by name.
(3) Use a format. If the permission is important, type the request individually.
(4) Make a file folder for each negotiation, including all pertinent information: name, address, phone number of publisher, the name of the contact (if any), a copy of the work from which permission is requested.
(5) When negotiation has been completed, forward a copy of the signed agreement to the user and keep one copy in the folder.

In any institution in which permissions are necessary, an administrator should be responsible for these kinds of uses. He or she could serve as a copyright clearinghouse for faculty members. This ensures that the procedures are simple, efficient, and legal. By having one person responsible, the institution could be better protected from lawsuits and replication of effort.

This practice would help in other ways, as well. The administrator could advise faculty on photocopying questions.[7] He or she could oversee a centralized duplicating center to make sure that the law is followed. Since cumulative uses are something individual teachers cannot be aware of, but for which institutions are responsible, this person would be in a position to view total faculty usage. Lastly, and most important, the faculty would be relieved of some of the burden of requests, and other paperwork and would be free to teach.

Part III

Library Use
of Copyrighted Materials

9

Library Reproduction Rights

Section 108 Overview

"Library reproduction rights" was a highly controversial part of the copyright law revision process. In part because of that, Section 108 is "(1) lengthy, (2) complex, (3) sometimes ambiguous, and (4) heavily embellished by legislative history."[1] The five-year study (108[i]) indicated that the Copyright Office found the library provision to be a "workable structural framework for obtaining a balance between creators' rights and users' needs...."[2] However, the American Library Association not only raised objection to the belief of the Register that a balance had been struck, it raised objection to the premise of the *Report* itself.[3]

Citing the First (right to know) and the Ninth (right to read) Amendments, it took "exception to the Register's constant referral in his report to 'creator's rights' and 'user's needs' " (see Appendix H).[4] Because of the continuing controversy and the lengthy and sometimes conflicting legislative history of this section, noted legal authorities Alan Latman and Robert Gorman observed that "it is no wonder that some libraries, preferring to avoid the mine field described above, are removing themselves from photocopying activities."[5]

Be that as it may, compliance with Section 108 provisions has proceeded at an orderly pace.[6] Notwithstanding the many definitional ambiguities inherent in this Section, it remains for the tests of time and technology to resolve these matters to a greater degree.[7] Technology is to be an area of study in the next five-year report.[8]

General Provisions of Section 108

For a library to be eligible for Section 108 photocopying, certain conditions must be met:

(1) *Noncommercial purpose*—the copy must be reproduced without any purpose of "direct or indirect commercial advantage" (Section 108[a][1]).[9]

(2) *Collection accessibility*—the collection must be available for use by others "doing research in a specialized field" (Section 108[a][2]).[10]

(3) *Copyright notice*—the work must include a "notice of copyright" (Section 108[a][3]).[11]

(4) *One article or other contribution per collection or issue*—for in-house or interlibrary loan purposes (Section 108[d]).[12]

(5) *The copy becomes "the property of the user"*—(Section 108 [d][1]).[13]

(6) *The copy's purpose is educational*—"private study, scholarship, or research" (Section 108[d][1]).[14]

(7) *A copyright warning is prominently displayed at order desk*— "a warning of copyright in accordance with the requirements that the Register of Copyrights shall prescribe by regulation" (Section 108[d][2]).[15] (See sample warning on page 69.)

In addition, the library, archive, or its employee must also:

(8) *Be unaware of related or concerted copying*—there must be no "substantial reason to believe" that multiple copies are being made, either "on one occasion or over a period of time" (Section 108[g][1]).[16]

(9) *Not engage in systematic copying*—no "systematic reproduction or distribution of single or multiple copies" (Section 108[g][2]).[17] (See Appendix F.)

(10) *Not engage in interlibrary arrangements in which the receiving library's purpose is to substitute for subscription or purchase of a work*—there must be no "purpose or effect that the library or archives receiving such copies or phonorecords for distribution does so in such aggregate quantities as to substitute for a subscription to or purchase of a work" (Section 108[g][2]).[18] (See Appendix F.)

Sample Warning Concerning Copyright Restrictions

The copyright law of the United States (Title 17, United States Code) governs the making of photocopies or other reproduction of copyrighted material.

Under certain conditions specified in the law, libraries and archives are authorized to furnish a photocopy or other reproduction. One of these specified conditions is that the photocopy or reproduction is not to be "used for any purpose other than private study, scholarship, or research." If a user makes a request for, or later uses, a photocopy or reproduction for purposes in excess of "fair use," that user may be liable for copyright infringement.

This institution reserves the right to refuse to accept a copying order if, in its judgment, fulfillment of the order would involve violation of copyright law.[19]

Other Photocopying Provisions

The librarian is frequently asked to make photocopies for employee or classroom use, as well as reproductions of slides, photographs, etc., for display purposes. However, the position of the librarian is somewhat different than for a teacher or other employees. While a teacher can make one or more copies for classroom use spur-of-the moment, the librarian may not.

> [F]or example, if a college professor instructs his class to read an article from a copyrighted journal, the school library would not be permitted, under subsection (g), to reproduce copies of the article for members of the class.[20]

The Register goes on to say that "it would be fair use for several students to make such copies."[21] For a librarian to do so would be considered "related or concerted" copying.[22] A librarian would be allowed to either make one copy or to make an excerpt provided that such a copy was according to Section 107, fair use.

The librarian may:

(1) *Make multiple copies* for a teacher if they meet the tests of brevity, spontaneity, and cumulative effect, or make copies of

10 percent of a performable unit of music or a phonograph record for educational purposes, as long as it appears not to be used for performance.[23] The one exception is last-minute emergency replacement copies for performance.[24]

(2) *Reproduce and distribute a copy of an entire out-of-print work*, if a copy can't be found at a fair price. The requirement is that a reasonable attempt should be made to acquire the work. If the work is deemed unreasonably high in regard to the original purchase price, or if it can't be found except through lengthy and expensive means, then a copy can be made.[25]

(3) *Copy an unpublished work* in the library's collection for preservation, security, or research use in another library open to the public.[26]

(4) *Copy to preserve a deteriorating published work* if reasonable effort has not produced an unused copy at a fair price.[27]

Any copies made should be sold without a profit and all copies should include the copyright notice where clearly visible.[28] If the librarian has a reason to believe that a copy is part of an attempt to accumulate copies then he or she should refuse to make a copy.[29] With few exceptions, copies may not be made of audiovisual, musical, pictorial, graphic, or sculptural works (see section on audiovisual works).[30] Lastly, while most librarians tend to think of copying as being only photocopying, the displaying of notices on microfiche and microfilm printers, reprographics, and photographic devices is also necessary.

Interlibrary Loan

Congress left the interlibrary loan question to the Commission on New Technological Uses of Copyright Works.[31] The CONTU suggested that the borrowing library adhere to the "rule of five" — five articles per periodical for the past five calendar years.[32] The lending library must also include notice of copyright on photocopies and check to see if the requirements for the notice of compliance with the guidelines have been filled. If the request does not comply, the American Library Association recommends that the request be denied.[33] However, some lending libraries either fill the request with a warning or call the borrowing library and ask for this information.[34]

The law permits libraries and archives to reproduce and distribute materials for interlibrary loan provided there is no substantial aggregate use by one or more individuals, and there is no systematic distribution of multiple copies. Obviously, conditions such as these require institutional discretion according to subscription policies and usage, yet, since the law has gone into effect, few interlibrary loans have gone beyond the five-copy limit on photocopied journals.[35] Some types of photocopying in certain classes of libraries have either increased slowly or even decreased since the law went into effect.[36]

The terms "related and concerted" and "systematic" reproduction or distribution of interlibrary loan materials have been a source of disagreement for librarians and their counsel due to the apparent inability of legislators to define them.[37]

The Register of Copyrights in the 1983 *Report* enumerated the guidelines (Subsection 208[g][2]) in a different manner to draw attention to the major points of the House guidelines[38]:

(1) The guidelines of the *House Report* were intended to cover "the most frequently encountered interlibrary case" — obtaining photocopies of articles published within five years prior to the request.

(2) The meaning of (g)(2) provision for older works will be left open to later interpretation.

(3) "The guidelines don't apply to entities that exist to make and distribute photocopies from a central source."

(4) The "aggregate substitution quantity" is "six or more copies of one or more articles from a given title during a calendar year."

(5) No more than five copies from a work during a calendar year for other (d) materials.

(6) If the library has a subscription to a periodical or a copy of other (d) materials, but the works are not available, then the copying is considered "local" rather than ILL.

(7) A photocopy can only be requested instead of an ILL if the requesting library could have supplied the copy from its own collection, but the work was unavailable for copying.

(8) Only requests accompanied by representations that the requesting library is complying with interlibrary loans can be filled.

(9) Requesting libraries must maintain records on the disposition of all requests governed by the guidelines "until the third calendar year after the year in which the request was made."[39]

The "rule of five" does not apply to ILL requests made by libraries which have entered subscriptions to the works of which a patron desires a copy.[40]

Records should be kept until December 31 of the third calendar year from which the request was made. For example, if a request was made January 23, 1986, the records should be kept until December 31, 1989. The requests must be kept in the same order on which the loan was made until that third calendar year. Information contained in the record should be summarized before it is destroyed. This summary should be in compliance with the five-year review mandated in the copyright law.[41]

Photocopying in For-Profit Libraries

For-profit libraries have greater restrictions placed upon uses of copyrighted materials, even though the library itself may function much the same as in any nonprofit institution (*Report of the Register of Copyrights*, 1983). The distinction between libraries which do and those libraries which do not qualify for Section 108 exemptions is "still a matter of dispute" according to the Register of Copyrights 1983 *Report*.[42] The Association of Authors and Publishers (AAP) believe that corporate libraries should consider the copying procedure adopted by Squibb and American Cyanamid for resolving some photocopying issues in companies with "extensive research facilities."[43]

The issue of whether or not for-profit libraries qualify for 108 privileges hinges mainly on the extent to which the "substantial majority" of its collection is "sufficiently open or accessible" either to the public or to unaffiliated persons doing research in a specialized field, including its competitors.[44] Restrictions based on age or educational status may be made without a loss of privileges under Section 108. However, to qualify for 208 treatment (suspension from paying licensing fees for photocopying) "substantial portions of the collection" must be open.[45] Participation in a network or interlibrary loan arrangement with similar libraries is not considered sufficient for 108 inclusion.[46]

Isolated, spontaneous photocopying of single copies is covered by Section 108 even though the copy is made for employees within the course of their work.[47] Under Section 108, libraries in profit-making organizations would not be authorized to use a single subscription or copy to supply its employees with multiple copies of material relevant to their work; use a single subscription to systematically supply its employees, on request, with single copies of material relevant to their work; or use "interlibrary loan arrangements to obtain photocopies in such aggregate quantities as to substitute for subscription or puchase of materials needed by employees in their work."[48]

The settlements reached between Harper & Row Publishers, Inc., and the two companies—Squibb and American Cyanamid—were very similar. Both companies were sued by Harper & Row for payment of royalties on reproduced copies of copyrighted publications of Harper & Row's copyrighted works. Their settlement agreements may indicate rough guidelines for other such libraries.

Both companies initiated the arrangements below:

(1) Registration with the Copyright Clearance Center (CCC).
(2) Reproduction on central copying facilities and other attended copying equipment located on company premises must be recorded and reported to the CCC.
(3) While not requested by Harper & Row, notices were placed on or adjacent to specified floor machines and other unattended copying equipment that copies of copyrighted material were not to be made thereon, and must be made at designated central copying facilities and equipment.
(4) Copies received from outside sources, whether from interlibrary loans or document-supply sources of CCC copyrighted material, would also be reported.[49]

Unsupervised Photocopying Equipment

The library is not responsible for illegal photocopying when warnings or the danger of copyright infringement are displayed. This notice must be displayed prominently, in no less than 18-point type, or larger, on durable material. These signs can be purchased. If the librarian is requested to make a copy, or to loan it out, the request can be refused. It is sufficient that a staff member has reason to believe that a request for a copy from reserve is to be used illegally. The librarian does not have to ask how the material is to be used. Comments of the patron are enough. In addition, copying machines in the library should also have a notice like this one:

NOTICE
PHOTOCOPYING RESTRICTIONS

The copyright law of the United States (Title 17, United States Code) governs the making of photocopies or other reproductions of copyrighted materials. The person using this equipment is liable for copyright infringement.[50]

The library is not liable for illegal photocopying of reserve or other material made on unsupervised copiers. The meaning of "unsupervised" has not been clearly defined, but if a copier is in another room, or out of the view of the librarian, the librarian is not liable. There are different types of notices, but the notice should indicate that the institution is not liable for the copyright infringement of the patron on an unsupervised copier, and that the patron is responsible for violations of copyright law in that instance.

Reserve Room Photocopying

The legislative history of the 1976 Act indicates that the issue of library reserve photocopying "did not receive great attention during revision" and was not addressed in Section 108 of the act.[51] The Register's *Report*, the ALA, and the American Association of Law Libraries (AALL) agree that, unlike other library photocopying practices which are restricted, library photocopying of materials for reserve room use falls within the fair use provisions of Section 107 under the concept of the "library-as-agent."[52] "Reserve copying is legal only if authorized by the copyright owner or by Section 107."[53] The only specific recommendation made by the 1983 *Report* was that permission should be obtained for multiple-term retention of multiple reserve copies.[54] However, some libraries allow multiple-term retention, believing that "the guidelines forbid repeated *copying*, but nowhere forbid the repeated *use* of material."[55] Other legal commentators concur that reserve room services are an extension of classroom copying guidelines, yet few definite answers to the number of copies which can be placed on reserve can be provided.[56] With regard to the special needs of higher education, the Section 107 guidelines state that "there may be instances in which copying which does not fall within the guidelines stated below may nonetheless be permitted under the criteria of fair use."[57] It was also noted in the *Report* that both the Association of University Professors and the Association of American Law Schools strongly criticized the Section 107 guidelines as "too restrictive."[58] The *Report* noted that "the Committee believes the guidelines are a reasonable interpretation of the *minimum* standards of fair use."[59]

When placing multiple copies of fair use materials on reserve it has been recommended that the photocopies be identified as belonging to that faculty member and should include full bibliographic information and should bear a notice of copyright.[60] The ALA and the AALL believe that a reasonable number of copies in most instances will be six.[61] Other factors which permit more copies in the library reserve room situation are:

(1) The amount of material should be reasonable in relation to the total amount of material assigned for one term of a course taking into account the nature of the course, its subject matter and level, 17 U.S.C. 107 (1) and (3).

(2) The number of copies should be reasonable in light of the number of students enrolled, the difficulty and timing of assignments, and the number of other courses which may assign the same materials, 17 U.S.C. 107 (1) and (3).

(3) The material should contain a notice of copyright; see 17 U.S.C. 401.

(4) The effect of photocopying the material should not be detrimental to the market for the work. (In general, the library should own at least one copy of the work.) 17 U.S.C. 107 (4).[62]

Library Networks

The Register of Copyrights believes that library networks may not make use of Section 108, and doubts the applicability of Section 107.[63] However, the American Association of Law Libraries (AALL) believes that "the simple fact that libraries become members of networks does not necessarily preclude them from replication rights provided by Sections 107 and 108."[64] Because of the inability at present to form such large networks, thereby preventing any test of the issues at hand; the changes which will inevitably occur in the information field, both with respect to technology and payment systems; and the possible changes in attitude and case law that could change any ensuing Register's *Report* at the designated five-year intervals, the controversy and opinion that surrounds ILL in library networks could quite possibly change.

Newsletters

While fair use applies to copying small sections of newsletters (such as the table of contents), the *House Report* had these special comments:

> It is argued that newsletters, as distinguished from house organs and publicity or advertising publications, be given separate treatment. It is argued that newsletters are particularly vulnerable to mass photocopying, and that most newsletters have fairly modest circulations. Whether the copying of portions of a newsletter is an act of infringement or a fair use will necessarily turn on the facts of the individual case. However, as a general principle, it seems clear that *the scope of the fair use doctrine should be considerably narrower in the case of newsletters than in that of either mass-circulation periodicals or scientific journals....* Copying by a profit-making user of even a small portion of a newsletter may have a significant impact on the commercial market for the work.[65]

Libraries qualifying under Section 108 copying should follow fair use guidelines closely. For-profit libraries, except in isolated instances of photocopying, should monitor newsletter copying for the need for subscriptions or licensed use.

Selective Dissemination of Information

Routing tables of contents and selected articles for patrons as a library service is covered by this section. It is clear that photocopying of tables of contents as a regular service to patrons would be within fair use. Routing of selected articles to patrons through SDI service would be permissible so long as the service was requested by the patron and one subscription to a journal was not ordered and routed systematically to take the place of ordering several.

Libraries are not permitted to purchase one subscription to a journal and then route a large number of copies of an article to interested employees (a CCC license should be obtained for this purpose).[66] Some in-house copying is within fair use. However, neither the act nor the legislative history provides numerical guidelines on what constitutes copying in such large quantities as to be systematic copying. Careful record keeping of patron SDI requests will aid in determining if copying is within fair use (Section 107) and Library Photocopying Guidelines (Section 108).

Commercial Publishing of U.S. Government Works

Commercial publishing of uncopyrighted government works is an acceptable practice for certain publishers because of the limited exposure and printing of certain documents which have importance for selected populations. In most cases the commercial prices are at least twice as high as the prices the U.S.G.P.O. charges for the same documents.[67] The advantage of purchasing from a commercial publisher is the improved typesetting and paper quality more suitable for library or institutional use.

Should one not desire these features and, instead, prefer purchasing the original document, it is advisable to check authorship. If it is a government publication, it will be so noted. Since some government works are contracted, and thus eligible for copyright, the lack of a copyright mark will indicate that the work is a government work and has been previously published by the G.P.O.

10

Library Video
and Software Use

Motion Picture and Video Exhibition

Libraries that lend authorized (legally acquired) videos or films for patron use are within the copyright law, even if a nominal fee or a deposit is required for their use.[1] The Motion Picture Association of America (MPAA) has stated that "libraries which circulate cassettes for use at home do not infringe the Copyright Act."[2] However, should a borrower state that the tape will be used for exhibition at a public place, such as a civic group's presentation to the general public requiring admission, then the lender has the duty to inform the borrower that such a use may violate copyright law. While the librarians would not be held as direct infringers, they and or the institution could be held as contributory infringers. A contributory infringer is one who "must either actively operate or supervise the operation of the place wherein the performances occur, or control the content of the infringing program, and expect commercial gain ... and either direct or indirect benefit from the infringing performance."[3] The same situation would hold true if the borrower stated the intention to make a copy.

The ALA (*American Libraries*, February, 1986) recommends the following for loan and duplication:

Loan.
(1) Videotapes labelled "For Home Use Only" may be loaned to patrons for their personal use. They should not knowingly be loaned to groups for public performances.
(2) Copyright notice as it appears on the label of a videotape should not be obscured.

(3) Nominal user fees may be charged.

(4) If a patron inquires about a planned performance of a video-tape, he or she should be informed that only private uses of it are lawful.

(5) Video recorders may be loaned to a patron without fear of lia-bility even if the patron uses the recorder to infringe a copy-right. However, it may be a good idea to post notices on equip-ment which may be used for copying (even if an additional machine would be required) to assist copyright owners in pre-venting unauthorized reproduction.

Duplication. Under limited circumstances libraries may dupe a videotape or a part thereof, but the rules of §108 of the Copyright Revision Act of 1976, which librarians routinely use with respect to photocopying, apply to the reproduction.

Public Libraries. The American Library Association takes this position on in-library uses (*American Libraries*, February, 1986):

(1) Most performances of a videotape in a public room as part of an entertainment or cultural program, whether a fee is charged or not, would be infringing and a performance license is re-quired from the copyright owner.

(2) To the extent a videotape is used in an educational program conducted in a library's public room, the performance will not be infringing if the requirements for classroom use are met.

(3) Libraries which allow groups to use or rent their public meeting rooms should, as part of their rental agreement, require the group to warrant that it will secure all necessary performance licenses and indemnify the library for any failure on their part to do so.

(4) If patrons are allowed to view videotapes on library-owned equipment, they should be limited to private performances, i.e., one person, or no more than one family, at a time.

(5) User charges for private viewings should be nominal and directly related to the cost of maintenance of the videotape.

(6) Even if a videotape is labelled "For Home Use Only," private viewing in the library should be considered to be authorized by the vendor's sale to the library with imputed knowledge of the library's intended use of the videotape.

(7) Notices may be posted on video recorders or players used in the library to educate and warn patrons about the existence of the copyright laws, such as: MANY VIDEOTAPED MATERIALS

ARE PROTECTED BY COPYRIGHT. 17 U.S.C. §101. UN-
AUTHORIZED COPYING MAY BE PROHIBITED BY LAW.

The entertainment corporation MGM/UA commenced a licensing
system for library exhibition based on the number of card holders a
library has for a mutually agreed upon number of scheduled exhibitions
plus unlimited unscheduled showings, with rights and formulas varying
by institution.[4] The wide acceptance of videos may indicate that such
licensing for public performance (categories number 1 and number 4 of
the ALA statement, above) is a direction that motion picture distributors
would like to see taken. However, the categories outlined by the ALA
statement indicate that a broadbased licensing scheme for all in-library
exhibition is unacceptable.[5]

School Libraries. School librarians regularly purchase videos, set
up viewing schedules for teachers, and tape programs for classroom use
at the request of instructors according to the "Guidelines" (see
Appendix A). All these activities are legally permissible. Quite often,
however, there is confusion about labels on videos which state that a
use is for "Home Use Only." This is a cautionary label for those who
would tape programs for resale and who would tape illegally. These
labels are not applicable to most school library situations. A school
library that lends or shows a video it has purchased, in the course of
"systematic teaching activities," is not infringing copyright law.

However, should the librarian lend a tape to a teacher or student
with knowledge that the video will be duplicated for resale or public
exhibition (an infringement), then that librarian could be considered a
contributory infringer, just as for photocopies, computer software, etc.

Videos — Usage Examples

(1) A librarian is requested to make a copy of short segments of
commercial television programs for classroom teachers for instructional purposes on rare and timely issues, such as child abuse, teenage
alcoholism, etc. ***Yes,** provided that the guidelines were followed.
Should an instructor wish that the segment be kept in the library for use
in later classes it would be safest to request permission, since several
producers did not agree to the off-air taping guidelines. If the teachers
wished to have what might be termed "fair use" segments (brief,
illustrative of an idea or attitude) to be kept in the library this would
likely be permissible.

(2) Can a media center director/librarian send around a list of possible programs that a teacher might like to request for off-air taping? *No. Off-air taping should only be done at the request of the individual teacher.

The following six examples are from the ALA (*American Libraries*, February, 1986):

(3) A book discussion group meets in a classroom at the high school. May they watch a videotape of *The Grapes of Wrath*? *No. The discussion group is not made up of class members enrolled in a nonprofit institution, nor is it engaged in instructional activities, therefore the classroom exception would not apply. Any such performance would be an infringing public performance because it is a place where a group of persons larger than a family and its social acquaintances are gathered. Permission of the copyright owner should be sought.

(4) Same as 3, but the group meets at a public library. *Maybe. The performance may infringe because the library is open to the public and the audience would be a group larger than a family and friends outside of a nonprofit instructional program.

(5) A patron asks if he can charge his friends admission to watch videotapes at his home. *The library's duty in this situation is merely to state that the videotape is subject to the copyright laws. In fact, as long as the patron shows the videotape at home to family or social acquaintances the performance would not be a public one, and therefore not infringing even if they share the cost of the videotape rental.

(6) A patron asks if he can charge admission to the general public and show the videotape at a public place. *No, this is an infringement; however, the librarian's duty is the same as in the previous situation.

(7) A librarian learns that a patron is borrowing videotapes and using them for public performances. *Again, there is a duty to notify the patron that the material is subject to the copyright laws. There is room for a variety of approaches to this situation, but there is no legal reason to treat videotapes differently from any other copyrighted materials which are capable of performance. While there is no clear duty to refuse to lend, there is a point at which a library's continued lending with actual knowledge of infringement could possibly result in liability for contributory infringement.

(8) I have been asked to add pirated videos to the school's collection. If I accepted them, would I be legally responsible? *Yes, you would. Do not accept pirated copies of any media into the school's

collection. This also includes any copies made under the off-air guidelines which were not subsequently licensed. While it is possible to keep a small segment of a program for fair use purposes, "librarying" of complete unlicensed programs is prohibited. If the teacher or library media specialist is aware that an item is illegally made, then he or she, as a responsible party to the act, could be legally liable. In the event that a program was accepted (regardless of the medium) without the receiver's believing or having reason to believe an item was illegally made, then that person would have to accept the "burden of proof" that he or she did not know the program was illegal. In such a case there would be no fine. This is called the "innocent infringer" provision.

Library Software Use

There are many aspects to the problem of illegal copying of software programs used in the library. As with unsupervised photo-copying (Section 108), the librarian can reduce liability for illegal copying of disks if a sign is displayed near the computer stating that the making of a copy of copyrighted materials is illegal. If the librarian has reason to believe that illegal copying is intended then it is the duty of that person to withhold the disk for lending purposes (Section 108[g]). If such an illegal use is made with the full knowledge of the librarian, then he or she becomes liable, because another's infringing was furthered.[6] If willful infringement is proved, then in addition to actual (based on profits made from the infringement) or statutory (court-imposed) damages up to $50,000, the court could also award court costs and attorney's fees to the losing party.

The law does provide a measure of grace for the well-intentioned. In a situation in which the librarian had no reason to believe that the use of a disk by a patron would be infringing, there would be no fine (Section 504[c]). However, the accused would have to sustain the burden of proving that she or he was innocent of any wrongdoing. This is called the "innocent infringer" provision.

Loan. The ALA (*American Libraries*, February, 1986) recommends these steps when loaning software:

(1) Copyright notice placed on a software label should not be obscured.

(2) License terms, if any, should be circulated with the software package.

(3) An additional notice may be added by the library to assist copyright owners in preventing theft. It might read: SOFTWARE PROTECTED BY COPYRIGHT, 17 U.S.C. §101. UNAUTHORIZED COPYING IS PROHIBITED BY LAW.

(4) Libraries generally will not be liable for infringement committed by borrowers.

School Library Use and Loan. Micros are being used for instruction, teacher checkout of popular classroom programs, student checkout of tutorial disks and other programs, database searching, and a host of other uses that have ethical and legal implications. With the number of computers in public schools having doubled in each of the past three years and expected to double again in each of the next four, controversies have risen over backups, multiple loading of disks, the reserve function, disk copying for teachers, student disk checkout, and the use of unsupervised micros located in the library media center.

These problems were punctuated by a recent action instituted by the International Communications Industries Association (ICIA), representing many of the smaller software publishing houses, against an Ohio school district for illegal (settled out of court) copying.[7] In any such case the district, its officers, and individual employees would be named. The school library media specialist, as director of a central repository and charged with the control of software dissemination, could very likely be included in such a suit as a "contributory infringer" if he or she had knowledge that the software was used for illegal copying.

Just as with the Motion Picture Association of America and the American Publishing Association, the ICIA is now sending out investigators when reports of illegal copying are made. The intention of the ICIA is not, however, as Kenton Pattie (ICIA's senior staff vice president) says, to pursue prosecution but to encourage proper use through public awareness efforts.[8]

There are a variety of ways to deal with the problem of potential infringement. Some schools have adopted the ICCE policy of requiring teachers who use school equipment to sign statements to the effect that they will comply with copyright laws, educate students about the legal and ethical problems caused by illegal use of software, purchase or lease software through a person authorized to sign software license agreements, be responsible for enforcing the terms of the district's policy and terms of licensing agreements, and take steps to prevent unauthorized copying or the use of unauthorized copies on school equipment. To add teeth to this policy, the ICCE also requires that "the legal or insurance protection of the District will not be extended to employees who violate copyright laws."[9] While both the teacher and the school district will likely be sued together, this clause means that if a teacher is sued for copyright infringement, the district will not pay for that person's legal fees.

The benefits of this or other such policies signed by all concerned would be to create better relations with producers when the district decides to preview or purchase software, as in the instance of San Diego County.[10] In the case of a district that had adopted such a policy, it could also be noted on the form the terms and conditions of the district policy on copyright and copying by personnel. The use of such a form is a gesture of commitment, one which could aid in negotiating previews, multiple copy discounts, etc.

The ICCE has recently updated its position on software policies.[11] In addition, the Office of Technology Assessment has published its study on *Intellectual Property Rights in an Age of Electronics and Information*, which assesses the effects of new information and communications technologies on United States law and practices regarding intellectual property.[12] The results of these two developments may affect computer use in the schools.

Library Software — Usage Examples

(1) Does a media center director have extra legal responsibilities? ***Yes,** Section 108 of the Copyright Act, which has to do with library photocopying, also has implications for software copying in a microcomputer lab or media center where one or more micros are housed. Legal liability can be reduced if a copyright sign is posted, similar to the one posted over the photocopier, stating that it is illegal to copy copyrighted materials.

NOTICE

It is illegal to copy or otherwise make duplicates of commercially produced software. Copying of such software will result in immediate disciplinary action and possible legal action by the publisher.

While younger children could not read this sign, the library media specialist or teacher could tell them about proper use of programs or use a program, such as "Pirates of the Soft Seas" (Microzine) to demonstrate proper use.

If the librarian has reason to believe that someone is copying a program illegally, then it is the librarian's duty to withhold the disk from circulation. If the librarian knows about and allows the illegal duplication of a copyrighted disk, then the librarian might share in the legal liability. Another thing to remember: making multiple copies of a program that was not designed for multiple-copy use probably is a violation of copyright law.

(2) A school library media specialist would like to make software available to lend to students. Can software be lent in such a way as to minimize illegal copying? ***Some** library media centers have adopted policies specifically for this purpose. Students who want to borrow software must take home a permission slip that they and their parents must sign. This form states that the student is responsible for ethical use of the software and promises not to make illegal copies. The parents also sign this statement and acknowledge their responsibility for their child's behavior. Not only is this policy a good way to inform unwitting parents of their children's responsibilities, but it also might reduce the school's liability.

If you would like to pursue checkout of copyrighted programs, a form should be made which would include: information on the legal use of copyrighted programs, a district policy statement on such use, a statement concerning any charges should a disk be returned damaged, and a statement that both the student and his or her parents will abide by copyright regulations and assume full responsibility for student checkout and use of such programs. This form should be signed by the parents and returned in order to commence software checkout.

Software checkout is being successfully implemented in both public and school libraries. While MECC (Minnesota Educational Computing Consortium) are the easiest of copyrighted programs to lend because of the relatively inexpensive multiple-copy license, public domain programs are also a good idea.

Another simple way to set up a software-lending program for students is to compile a library of public domain software. Public domain software offers many opportunities, because such programs generally are easy to copy and because a wide array is available.

Although quite a bit of public domain software exists, little of it is produced specifically for schools and colleges. For a software-lending library, however, such programs might be quite useful. Books exist that are devoted to obtaining free software. One is *How to Get Free Software*, by Alfred Glossbrenner, and another is *The Free Software Catalog and Directory*, by Robert Froelich. Local users' groups also often offer free software.

There is one excellent public domain software-exchange program that exists specifically for educators. Called Softswap, it is run by the Microcomputer Center in the San Mateo County Office of Education in Redwood City, California. (For details, write to Ann Lathrop, San Mateo County Office of Education, 333 Main Street, Redwood City CA 94063.) Another high-quality public domain software company is the Computer Learning Center, POB 110876, Tacoma WA 98411.

Finally, many school systems and higher education institutions have adopted the model policies on software copyright formulated by the International Council for Computers in Education. (For a copy, write to ICCE, 1787 Agate Street, Eugene OR 97403.)

(3) A teacher requested the librarian to place on reserve pirated copies of software programs. Could the librarian be held liable for placing them on reserve?*Yes. The librarian could be held for contributory infringement and the institution could also be held liable for infringement.[13]

(4) I have begun to do on-line searching for teacher and student use. The modem that I purchased allows me to download the search at cheaper evening rates and then present the search to the teacher/administrator/student the next day. Is this legal? *Yes, as long as downloading is covered in the database vendor's agreement. Wilsonline, DIALOG, and BRS all have a statement concerning downloading. If the vendor does not, then downloading a record for delayed search purposes and then discarding it immediately would be considered fair use and is clearly not grounds for infringement. Copying a substantial portion of a database, such as most of any databases available on Wilsonline, would be difficult to do, and would be an infringement.

The line where fair use ends and infringement begins has yet to be drawn. The fact that downloading license agreements typically allow temporary storage at no extra charge or at a minimal charge indicates the widespread practice of downloading for late use because of time constraints and the reluctance of database vendors to pursue an infringement action. Frequently, the conditions are that such storage is within the terms of the agreement, provided that it is used only with the organization and that there is no intent for resale or transfer to other than the downloading site.

(5) I have a micro located in our library media center for student and teacher use. Lately I have noticed students bringing in disks and trying to make copies. What should I do? ***There are several** possible solutions. Four comparatively simple steps to take first are to explain the need for ethical behavior and give examples of both ethical and unethical behavior when classes visit through the year, and make it clear that there will be suspension of privileges should unethical behavior occur. Also, post a copyright or similar notice near the micro concerning illegal copying. Such a notice relieves the library media specialist of legal liability to some extent when he or she is unable to monitor its use all the time (just as with unsupervised photocopiers; see Example 1 immediately above). The librarian should refuse to let the students use the micro until a permission slip has been signed by their parents stating that their child will not do illegal copying, and should make up sign-up sheets so that use can be better controlled.

The following five examples are from the ALA (*American Libraries*, February, 1986):

(6) A math teacher puts a copy of Visicalc on reserve in the school library. The disk bears no copyright notice. May the library circulate it? *The disk ought to bear the copyright notice, but whether it is the library's legal duty to require that one be affixed is unclear. Individual library reserve policies may govern this situation—it's probably a good idea to require that the appropriate notices be affixed prior to putting the copy on reserve. Further, the lack of copyright notices may put the library on notice that this is a copy rather than the original program. If the original is retained by the teacher as an archival copy (i.e., not used) there is no problem. If not, then the reserve copy is an unauthorized copy and its use would violate the copyright laws and most license agreements. While the library might not be legally liable in this situation it would be wise to establish a policy for placing materials on reserve which prevents this.

(7) May the library make an archival copy of the Visicalc program on its reserve shelf? ***Usually yes.** Section 117 permits the owner of the software to make or authorize the making of one archival copy. If the teacher who put the program on reserve has not made one, she or he may permit the library to do so. Remember, most license agreements and the copyright laws permit the making of one archival copy.

(8) Same as 7, except the reserve copy is damaged. May the library

make another copy (assuming it has the archival copy) for circulation? *Yes, the purpose of an archival copy is for use as a backup in case of damage or destruction. The library may then make another archival copy to store while circulating the other.

(9) Same as 8, except the reserve copy is stolen. *Perhaps. It is not clear whether the purpose of a backup copy includes replacement in the event of theft but arguably it does. However, §108(c) permits reproduction of audiovisual works (which includes many computer programs) in the event of damage, loss, or theft *only* if a replacement may not be obtained at a fair price. Further, some license agreements require that archival copies be destroyed when possession (not ownership) of the original ceases. Therefore a replacement copy may need to be purchased. A safe course is to consult the software vendor.

(10) When the teacher retrieves his or her copy of the program may the library retain the archival copy? *No. When possession of the original ceases, the archival copy must be transferred with the original or destroyed. If it is returned with the original, the teacher would not be permitted to make additional copies—he or she would have an original and the archival copy. Most license agreements contain similar provisions.

(11) Why should we adopt a copyright policy? Maybe we should just wait until matters become clearer. *I wouldn't advise waiting. All things being equal, should a producer have to decide which district would be best to make an example suit or a "test case," the most obvious choice would be the district without a policy. This is presumably because those districts which do not have a copyright policy indicate their unwillingness to address the issue and thereby treat the problem. Such a course of action was used in a case against New York University in 1982 and in the recent one in Ohio. Much of the information which decides whether an investigator will be sent in is anecdotal, that is, either witnessed by a representative or by informed sources. The old adage that it is "better to be safe than sorry" still rings true.

Part IV

Bibliography, References, Simplified Guidelines

Bibliography/Resource Guide

General Copyright Resources

The materials listed below are provided as a highly selective guide. The references for each chapter provide numerous other sources.

BNA's Patent, Trademark & Copyright Journal (weekly periodical). Cases and information in all areas for attorneys and others.

The copyright directory. (1985). Copyright Information Services, POB 1460-D, Friday Harbor WA 98250. Provides names, phone numbers, and addresses of persons to contact for copyright, permissions, and licensing information in many areas.

The copyright game resource guide. Becker, G., Director of Media Services, Seminole County Public Schools, Sanford, Fla. (1770 Blackmon Court, Longwood FL 32779). Game that helps players to better understand copyright in an enjoyable way.

Copyright handbook, 2d ed. Johnston, D. (1982). New York: R.R. Bowker. Easy-to-read digest of copyright law for the layman.

Copyright in the eighties, 2d ed. Latman, A., Gorman, R., & Ginsburg, J. (1985). Charlottesville, Va.: Michie Bobbs-Merrill. Treats all aspects of copyright for the legal practitioner in a readable form that can be used by laymen. Cases and relevant documents are included.

Copyright Management (monthly periodical). Available at a few libraries in the U.S., this journal provides a synopsis of the latest information on copyright in all areas for the layman.

Copyright policy development: A resource book for educators. Vlek, C.W. (1986). Copyright Information Services, POB 1460-D, Friday Harbor WA 98250. Information on how to construct workable copyright policies.

Fair use and free inquiry; copyright law and the new media. Lawrence, J.S., & Timberg, B. (1980). Norwood, N.J.: Ablex. Essays by various educators on copyright law as it applies to educational uses.

"How to research copyright law." Chee, L. (1977). *Law Library Journal*, **70**, 171–183. Provides information necessary to do research.

Nimmer on copyright: A treatise on the law of literary, musical, and artistic property, and the protection of ideas (4 vols.), revised edition. 1978–1985. Nimmer, M. New York: Mathew Bender. Nimmer was considered the preeminent authority on copyright before his recent death. The format is looseleaf. 1986 edition being revised by David Nimmer.

Library of Congress Mailings and Information

It is anticipated that regulations may change in the future, with the enormous progress being made by on-line retrieval mechanisms, consortia, micrographics, etc. Aside from the information that can be obtained from library periodicals, the Copyright Office also has a free periodic mailing list that can be requested on subjects of interest by phoning (202) 287-8700 or by writing to Information and Publications Section, LM-455, Copyright Office, Library of Congress, Washington DC 20559. The Copyright Office also answers questions by phone. Trained information specialists will answer copyright questions on a phone-in basis. Depending on the request—such as music, video, print materials, etc.—they will often send appropriate documents and information free of charge.

A copyright forms hotline is also available for registration: (202) 287-9100.

Free from the U.S. Copyright Office are Circular R1 *Copyright Basics*, Circular R2 *Publications on Copyright*, Circular R2b

Bibliographies, Selected, Circular R21 *Reproduction of Copyrighted Works by Educators and Librarians,* and the *Copyright Act of 1976.*

Video Copyright Resources

In making and acquiring legal copies of video and off-air programs, there are some very good resources that offer help for permissions, sample educational program inquiry forms, policies, services, and directories. The materials listed below are provided as a selected guide to copyright for the layman. The list is not meant to be complete. For other sources, please consult the chapter references.

EITV (Educational and Industrial Television) (monthly). C.S. Tepfer Pub. Co., 51 Sugar Hollow Road, Danbury CT 06810. An annual directory of program sources is provided and listed according to the audience and content. While there is a subscription fee per year, a free subscription may be obtained if one is in a position of responsibility for acquisition or production, etc.

How to acquire legal copies of video programs. Johnson, B. (1984). Learning Resource Center, San Diego State University, San Diego CA 92182. Has information on free programs, resources for "off-air" licensing opportunities, sources for individual programs, sample forms, information on how to approach producers for copies, negotiation, and a recommended resource library.

NICEM index to educational videotapes. National Information Center for Educational Media, POB 40130, Albuquerque NM 87196; (800) 421-8711. Has listings of over 60,000 titles, and may also be accessed by number 46 on DIALOG (additional info from file 46).

Off-air videotaping in education: Copyright issues, decisions, implications. Sinofsky, E. (1984). New York: R.R. Bowker. Discussion of issues involved in off-air taping, including a list of producers who do not adhere to the educational guidelines.

PBS Video. 475 L'Enfant Plaza SW, Washington DC 20024; (800) 424-7963 — information, (800) 344-3337 — ordering and customer service. Puts out the *PBS Video Catalog* free of charge and arranges for licensing of "off-air" copies of programs for $125 for most programs. For extended instructional television off-air recording retention rights, PBS Educational Services (800-257-2578) can be contacted. It publishes a monthly newsletter, *PBS Video News*, at no charge. Some of the programs include teachers' guides.

Sat Guide: Cable's Satellite Magazine. Sat-Guide, POB 29, Boise ID 83707. Provides listings of programmers, programming categories (movies, educational, ethnic), contact persons, addresses and affiliate costs, if any.

Satellite Directory (annual). Phillips Publishing, 7811 Montrose Road, Potomac MD 20854. Programming services, program descriptions and formats, business and information services, satellite operators, etc., are provided.

The Television Licensing Center, a subsidiary of Films Incorporated, through its monthly (except in summer) newsletter — the *TLC Guide* — gives extensive information about off-air taping opportunities and handles royalty payments and record keeping of licensing of tapes which the institution wishes to retain. This service is provided free to members. Each video licensed is $125 per hour program. Membership is free. 1144 Wilmette Avenue, Wilmette IL 60091; (800) 323-4222. Sometimes teachers' guides are available at a nominal fee.

Video/copyright seminar (audiocassette). Miller, J.K. (1986). Copyright Information Services, POB 1460-C, Friday Harbor WA 98250. Discusses off-air taping, policy development, licensing, satellite taping, etc., for the educational user.

Video source book. Gale Research Company, Book Tower, Detroit MI 48226. Has synopses and evaluations (including sources) of over 40,000 videos from 800 sources.

World Satellite Almanac: The Complete Guide to Satellite Transmission and Technology (annual). POB 43, Boise ID 83707. Inexpensive guide to all aspects of satellite programming. Includes sections which describe the mechanics of satellite dishes and programming. Programmers are included.

Computer Software Copyright Resources

The materials listed below are provided as a selected guide to copyright for the layman. The list is not meant to be complete. For other sources, please consult the references for each chapter.

Copyright: A practical guide to microcomputer licenses. Strauss, S., General Counsel to the International Communications Industries Association (ICIA). (1986). Copyright Information Services, 440 Tucker Road, Friday Harbor WA 98250. Includes useful information on acquiring site licenses, "shrink-wrap" agreements, etc.

How to copyright software. Salone, M.J. (ed. by S. Elias). (1984). Berkeley, CA: Nolo Press. This book has good information for the reader, as well as explanations of numerous facets of copyright.

Legal care for your software; a step-by-step guide for computer software writers. Remer, D. (1982). Berkeley, CA: Nolo Press. Much information on copyright and software for the writer as well as the user.

"Look both ways before copying." Talab, R. (Feb./March 1985). *TechTrends*, pp. 28–30. Question and answer format for microcomputer software and hardware questions.

Sample corporate policies on software piracy. ADAPSO (Association of Data Processing Service Organizations), 1300 N Seventeenth Street, Arlington VA 22209; (703) 522-5055. Free. Provides business and educational sample policies.

Software quality and copyright: Issues in computer-assisted instruction. (1984). Washington, DC: Association for Educational Communications and Technology (AECT). A timely discussion of copyright and educational use of software, as well as guidelines.

"Untangling the copyright issues." Williams, C. (Nov./Dec. 1985). *Electronic Learning*, pp. 47 + . A survey of publishers and their various stances on licensing is presented, including names and addresses.

Library Copyright Resources

The list below is not intended to be complete. For additional resources see the chapter references.

"Copyright and libraries—a librarian's perspective." Lucker, J.K.
(1983). In J. Baumgarten & A. Latman (eds.), *Corporate copyright and information practices.* New York: Practicing Law Institute. This chapter has good information on photocopying in
libraries in for-profit institutions.

Copyright handbook (AALL Publications Series). Heller, J., & Wiant,
S.K. (1984). Littleton, Colo.: Fred B. Rothman. While designed
for use by the AALL, this book is very good for most uses of
materials in libraries.

"Library and classroom use of copyrighted videotapes and computer
software." Reed, M.H., & Stanek, D.J. (Feb. 1986). *American
Libraries.* This is the first statement by the ALA on its position
regarding uses of this media since the 1977 book (immediately
above).

Microcomputer software policies in ARL libraries. The Association of
Research Libraries SPEC Kit #123, ARL, Office of Management
Studies, 1527 New Hampshire Avenue, NW., Washington, DC
20036. The kit includes information about special limitation to acquisition and circulation, software selection, and other topics.

*Report of the Register of Copyrights: Library reproduction of copy-
righted works* (17 U.S.C. 108). Copyright Office, Library of Congress. (Jan. 1983). Washington, D.C.: U.S. Government Printing
Office. This is the first report, presented at five-year intervals, on
library uses of copyrighted works. See also the response of the
ALA in the Appendix.

"Warnings of copyright for use by libraries and archives." Copyright
Office. (March 1983). *Circular R 96* (Section 201.14). Washington,
D.C.: U.S. Government Printing Office. This contains warning
signs on violation of copyright law suitable for posting.

Chapter Notes

Chapter 1

1. Henry, N. *Copyright–information technology–public policy* (2 vols.). New York: Marcel Dekker, 1975.
2. Ibid.
3. Gipe, G. *Copyright and the machine nearer to the dust.* Baltimore: Williams & Wilkins, 1967.
4. Nimmer, M. "Does copyright abridge the first amendment guarantees of free speech and press?" *UCLA Law Review*, 17, 1180-1204. 1970.
5. Patterson, L. *Copyright in historical perspective.* Nashville: Vanderbilt University Press, 1968.
6. White, H. (ed.). *The copyright dilemma.* Chicago: American Library Association, 1978.
7. Reitz, N. "Williams & Wilkins: The impact of technology on copyright." *Los Angeles Bar Bulletin*, pp. 445-472. 1973.
8. Nimmer, M. *Cases and materials on copyright: a treatise on the law of literary, musical, and artistic property, and the protection of ideas* (4 vols.). New York: Mathew Bender, 1981.
9. Marke, J. *Copyright and intellectual property.* New York: Fund for the Advancement of Education, 1967.
10. U.S. Congress, House, Judiciary Committee. *Report No. 94-1476. Report together with additional views (to accompany S. 22)* (94th Congress, 2nd Session). Washington, D.C.: U.S. Gov. Printing Office, Sept. 3, 1976, pp. 130-133.
11. *Williams & Wilkins Co. v. United States*, 172 U.S.P.Q. 670 (Comm'r Ct. Cl. 1972), rev'd 487 f2d. 1345, 1363 (Ct.Cl. 1973), aff'd. by an equally divided court, 420 U.S. 376 (1975).
12. U.S. Congress, House, Judiciary Committee. *Report No. 94-1476. Report together with additional views (to accompany S. 22)* (94th Congress, 2nd session). Washington D.C.: U.S. Gov. Printing Office, Sept. 3, 1976, pp. 53-56.
13. *HR. 94-1476*, p. 53.
14. Douglas, J. "Copyright as it affects instructional development." *Audio visual Instruction*, December, 1974, pp. 37-38.
15. Nimmer, M. *Cases and materials on copyright: a treatise on the law of*

literary, musical, and artistic property, and the protection of ideas (4 vols.). New York: Mathew Bender, 1981.

16. Black, J. *Black's Law Dictionary*, 1967.
17. H.R. 94-1476, *Ibid.*, p. 60.
18. H.R. 94-1476, *Ibid.*, p. 57.
19. H.R. 94-1476, *Ibid.*, pp. 61–65.
20. H.R. 94-1476, *Ibid.*, p. 120.
21. Wincor, R. *Rights contracts in the communications media.* New York: Law & Business, 1982.
22. Polking, K., and L. Meramus. *Law and the Writer.* Cincinnati: Writer's Digest Books, 1981.
23. H.R. 94-1476, p. 52.
24. Beil, N. *The writer's legal and business guide.* New York: Arco Publishing, 1984.
25. Latman, A., Gorman, R., and Ginsburg, J. *Copyright for the eighties* (2nd ed.). Charlottesville, VA: Michie Bobbs-Merrill, 1985, p. 514.

Chapter 2

1. *Folsom v. Marsh*, 9 F. Cas. 342 (C.C.D. Mass. 1841) (No. 4, 901).
2. See: Chafee, Z., Jr. (1945), *Reflections on the law of copyright* (Columbia L. Review 503, 511); and Latman, A. (1960), *Fair use of copyrighted works* (Copyright Law Revision Study No. 14). Dr. Jerome Miller also provides information on copyright via Copyright Information Services, 440 Tucker Rd., Friday Harbor, WA 98250, which publishes monographs on copyright, such as *The copyright directory* and *Using copyrighted videocassettes in classrooms and libraries* for the education and library audiences.
3. Cohen, S. (1955). Fair use in the law of copyright. *American Society of Composers and Publishers Copyright Law Symposium, 43*, 38–49.
4. *Farmer v. Calvert Lithographic Co.*, 8 Fed. Cas. 1022, No. 4, 651 at 1026 (C.C.E.D. Mich. 1872); *Macmillan Co. v. King*, 223 F. 862 (1914); *Henry Holt & Co. v. Liggett & Meyers Tobacco Co.*, 23 F. Supp. 302 (E.D. Pa. 1938); *Rosemont Enterprises, Inc., v. Random House*, 366 F. 2d 303 (2d Cr., 1966), cert. denied, 385 U.S. 1009, 17 Ed. 2d 546, 87 Sup. Ct. 714 (1967); *Williams & Wilkins v. the United States*, 172 U.S.P.Q. 670 (Comm'r C. Cl. 1972), rev'd 487 F. 2d 1345 (Ct. Cl. 1973), aff'd by an equally divided court, 420 U.S. 376 (1975); *Wihtol v. Crow*, 309 F. 2d 777 (8th Cir. 1963); *Dallas Cowboy Cheerleaders, Inc., v. Scoreboard Posters, Inc.*, 600 F. 2d 1184 (1979); *Universal City Studios, Inc., v. Sony Corporation of America*, 480 F. Supp. 429, 203 U.S.P.Q. 656 (C.D. Cal. 1979), rev'd in part, aff'd in part, 659 F. 2d 963, 211 U.S.P.Q. 761, 551 PTCJ D-1 (9th Cir. 1981), rev'd 52 U.S.L.W. 4090 (1984). See also Copyright fair use—case law and legislation (1969), *Duke Law Journal*, pp. 73–109; and Lawrence, M. (1982), *Fair use: Evidence of change in a traditional doctrine* (27 ASCAP Copyright Law Symposium 71). While the above cases were ruled in favor of either private parties or educational defendants, two other cases ruled against educational defendants:

Wihtol v. Crow, 199 F. Supp. 682, 132 U.S.P.Q. 392 (S.D. Iowa 1961), rev'd 309 F. 2d 777, 135 U.S.P.Q. 385 (8th Cir. 1962), in which a church choir director incorporated a copyrighted hymn in a new arrangement which was publicly performed; and *Encyclopaedia Britannica Educational Corporation v. Crooks*, 447 F. Supp. 243 (W.D.N.Y. 1978), in which defendants videotaped a number of copyrighted educational films without permission and distributed them to member school districts via catalog. However, case law and the 1976 Act have granted broad application to the fair use doctrine.

5. U.S. Constitution. Art. I, sec. 8, cl. 8.
6. I. Stat. 124.
7. For discussions of the purpose of fair use in the public interest see *Rosemont Enterprises, Inc., v. Random House, Inc.* and *Time, Inc., v. Bernard Geis Assoc.*, 293 F. Supp. 130 (S.D.N.Y. 1968). Latman, Gorman, & Ginsburg (1985), *Copyright in the eighties* (2nd ed.), Charlottesville, Va.: Michie Bobbs-Merrill, includes a discussion of the first amendment issues raised most recently in copyright and fair use considerations. Other discussions on this topic are M. Nimmer, Does copyright abridge the First Amendment guarantees of free speech and press, *UCLA Law Review, 17*, 1180–1204; and *Triangle Publications, Inc., v. Knight Ridder Newspapers, Inc.*, 626 F. 2d 1171 (5th Cir. 1980), which held that the defense of fair use and the First Amendment are separate. See also Rosenfield, The Constitutional dimension of "fair use" in copyright law, *The Notre Dame Lawyer, 50*, 790–807; and *Harper & Row Publishers, Inc., v. Nation Enterprises*, 557 F. Supp. 1067 (S.D.N.Y. 1983), rev'd 753 F. 2d 195 (2d Cir. 1983), cert. granted (U.S. 1984), in which the Copyright Act, the court declared, "was not intended to provide such a private monopoly of act at the expense of the public's need to be informed."
8. Seltzer, L. (1978). *Exemptions and fair use in copyright, the rights tensions in the 1976 copyright act* (p. 36). Cambridge, MA: Harvard University Press. See also Photocopying and fair use: An examination of the economic factors in fair use (1977), *Emory Law Journal, 26*, 849–884.
9. *Henry Holt & Co. v. Liggett & Meyers Tobacco Co.* involved the use of three sentences for a commercial advertisement. *Karll v. Curtis Publishing Co.*, 39 F. Supp. 836, 51 U.S.P.Q. (E.D. Wis. 1941) turned upon the "purpose for which the letters were included in the book" as well as the other fair use factors.
10. National Association of College and University Business Officers (NACUBO). (1978, July 31). *Special report 1977–1979*. Washington, DC: NACUBO.
11. See National Commission of New Technological Uses of Copyrighted Works (CONTU) (1978, July 31), *Final report*, Washington, DC: U.S. Government Printing Office; and Toward a unified theory of copyright infringement for an advanced technological era (1982), *Harvard Law Review, 96*, 450, for discussions of new technology and copyright. Henry, N. (1975), *Copyright, information technology, public policy* (2 vols.), New York: Marcel Dekker, discusses the effect of "electronic publishing" on the intellectual property from a marxist perspective and explores policy implications for information dissemination. Steele, K. (Ed.) (1984), *Electronic publishing: Old issues in a new industry*, New

York: Practicing Law Institute, offers presentations on the influence of the developments of various media on copyright law. A relevant case on technology is *Twentieth Century Music Corp. v. Aiken*, 356 F. Supp. 271, 177 U.S.P.Q. 751 (W.D. Pa. 1973), rev'd 500 F. 2d 127, 182 U.S.P.Q. 388 (3d Cir. 1974), aff'd 422 U.S. 151, 186 U.S.P.Q. 65 (1975), which held that "[w]hen technological change has rendered its literal terms ambiguous, the Copyright Act must be construed in light of [its] basic purpose." *Universal City Studios, Inc., v. Sony Corp. of America*, 480 F. Supp. 429 (C.D. Ca. 1979), discusses copyright in light of developing technology. *Apple Computer, Inc., v. Franklin Computer Corp.*, 714 F. 2d 1240, 219 U.S.P.Q. 113 (1983), established that computer operating systems embodied in ROM are copyrightable and illustrates the developments involving copyright and new technology.

12. Johnston, D. (1982). *Copyright handbook* (2nd ed.). New York: R.R. Bowker. See *House report 97-1476* (pp. 65–66) (1976, September 3), Washington, DC: U.S. Government Printing Office, for an explanation of the codified doctrine.

13. See note #9. M. Nimmer notes that the "statute gives no guidance as to the relative weight of the factors..." Nimmer, M. (1979). *Nimmer on copyright: A treatise of the law of literary, musical, and artistic works* (2nd ed., Vol. 3, Section 13.05[A]). St. Paul, MN: West Publishing. See note #8 for Seltzer's (1978) discussion of the importance of the economic aspect, also.

14. For discussions of the fair use factors, see Cohen, note #3, for a definitive analysis. Carnahan, in note #9, Chapter 3, explores eight aspects of these factors. R. Needham outlined 16 factors affecting fair use determinations in: Tape recording, photocopying, and fair use (1959), *American Society of Composers, Authors, and Publishers Copyright Law Symposium*, *10*, 75–103. See also D. Brooks' discussion of fair use factors in Appendix A: Helm, V. (1984), *Software quality and copyright: Issues in computer-assisted instruction* (pp. 116–121), Washington, D.C.: Association for Educational Communications and Technology. The amount of independent research in preparing a work has also been a criterion for determining fair use. When much independent research has been done, fair use has been accepted. See: *Hartford Printing Co. v. Hartford Directory & Publishing Co.*, 196 F. 332 (C.C.D. Conn. 1906); *Toksvig v. Bruce Publishing Co.*, 181 F. 2d 664 (7th Cir. 1950); and *Oxford Book Co. v. College Entrance Book Co.*, 98 F. 2d 688, 691 (2d Cir. 1938).

15. See *Thompson v. Gernsback*, 94 F. Supp. 453, 87 U.S.P.Q. 238 (1950), which affirmed that "scientific, legal, medical, and similar books or articles of learning" are granted greater use of copyrighted materials because of the purpose of their use and the intent for which it is made. A more recent case emphasizing this factor was *Triangle Publications v. Knight-Ridder Newspapers*, in which it was noted that the purpose of the use was the first factor to be considered. *Meeropol v. Nizer*, 560 F. 2d 1061, 195 U.S.P.Q. 273 (2d Cir. 1977), cert. denied, 434 U.S. 1013 (1978), found that the purpose for which a use was made of copyrighted letters was of most importance in finding the use to be fair. *Henry Holt & Co. v. Liggett & Meyers Tobacco Co.*, found that the use of three sentences for a

commercial venture (a pamphlet promoting cigarettes quoted from a book by Holt written for voice teachers) is afforded significantly less latitude than an educational or scholarly use. See also *Dr. Pepper Co. v. Sambo's Restaurants,* 517 F. Supp. 1202 (N.D. Tex. 1981), "any commercial use tends to cut against a fair use doctrine."

16. D. Hayes found that the second factor is the least used factor in determining fair use in: Classroom "fair use": A reevaluation (1978), *Bulletin of the Copyright Society of the U.S.A.*, *26*, 101–129. Analyses of copyright decisions involving educational or scholarly uses of materials show that the number of cases involving this type of work are relatively rare when compared with cases involving entertainment works, loosely categorized as popular fiction, music, film, etc. *Rosemont Enterprises, Inc., v. Random House, Inc.* discussed this criterion to some extent. *Henry Holt & Co. v. Liggett & Meyers Tobacco Co.* involved the use of scholarly work on voice to enhance a pamphlet designed to sell cigarettes. The use of the work "has cast reflections upon him the term 'commercialist' ... which has contributed to negate and deter the sale of his [Feldmerman's] book." The nature of the work and the profit motive of the use made of it amounted to infringement. See also *Harper & Row Pub., Inc., v. Nation Enterprises* and *Eckes v. Card Prices Update,* 736 F. 2d 85 (2d Cir. 1985). For a comprehensive discussion of the second factor, along with supporting cases, see Perry, W. (1985), The fair use privilege, in M. Goldberg (Ed.), *Copyright law 1985* (pp. 621–626), New York: Practicing Law Institute.

17. The criterion of "substantial taking" has been applied often. See *Ager v. Peninsular and Oriental Steam Navigation Company,* 26 C.D. 637 (1884), in which multiple copies were reproduced. *Addison Wesley Publishing Co. v. Brown,* 223 F. Supp. 219, 139 U.S.P.Q. 47 (1963), found "substantial" copying of another work. *Marcus v. Rowley,* 695 F. 2d 1171, CCH Cop. L. Rep. Section 25, 486 (9th Cir. 1983), found substantial copying, even with attribution, in a textbook for a cake decorating course in a nonprofit education institution to be an infringement. See: *Leon v. Pacific Telephone and Telegraph Company,* 91 F. 2d 484, 34 U.S.P.Q. 237 (9th Cir. 1937), in which the amount copied was seen as "wholesale copying and publication." *Macmillan Co. v. King,* 223 F. 862 (D. Mass. 1914), held that King, a tutor, made memoranda sheets which "were intended to outline all subject matter." See *Southwestern Bell Tel. Co. v. Nationwide Independent Directory Serv., Inc.,* 371 F. Supp. 900 (W.D. Ark. 1974), and *Wainwright Securities, Inc., v. Wall Street Transcript Corp,* 418 F. Supp. 620 (S.D.N.Y. 1976), aff'd 558 F. 2d 91 (2d Cir. 1977), cert. denied, 434 U.S. 1014 (1978). Parody is given wider latitude under the fair use doctrine. *Elsmere Music, Inc., v. NBC,* 482 F. Supp. 741 (S.D.N.Y.), aff'd 623 F. 2d 252 (2d Cir. 1980), held that copying parts of "I Love New York" as well as two of the four-word lyrics was a fair use because the parody "I Love Sodom" is afforded greater leeway. However, parody is not always a successful defense in an infringement suit. See *Loew's, Inc., v. Columbia Broadcasting System, Inc.*, 131 F. Supp. 165, 105 U.S.P.Q. 302 (S.D. Cal. 1955), aff'd sub nom, *Benny v. Loew's, Inc.*, 239 F. 2d 532, 112 U.S.P.Q. 11 (9th Cir. 1959),

aff'd per curiam by an equally divided court, 356 U.S. 43, 116 U.S.P.Q. 479 (1958).

18. In music, particularly, the qualitative aspect is most often found. See *Elsmere Music, Inc., v. NBC*, 482 F. Supp. 741 (S.D.N.Y.), aff'd 623 F. 2d 252 (2d Cir. 1980), in which copying the "heart" of a song ("I Love New York" used for a parody titled "I Love Sodom") was seen as fair use because of the greater leeway afforded parody. See also *Warner Bros. v. ABC*, 720 F. 2d 231 (2d Cir. 1983), 654 F. 2d 204 (2d. Cir. 1982).

19. Seltzer (1978), op cit. See also *Hill v. Whalen & Martell*, 220 F. 359, 18 Copy. Dec. 224 (S.D.N.Y. 1914), and *Folsom v. Marsh*; both found that infringement can be found when such a large amount is used that the value of the original could be lessened. As indicated by Seltzer (1978) and Cohen (1955), the effect of the use on the potential market is most often determined by balancing all of the factors. M. Nimmer (1979) described a "functional test" in which if a copy serves the function of the original, fair use might not be used as a defense. The effect of the copies being made afforded potential damage to the market of the originals in the *Universal City Studios, Inc., v. Sony Corporation of America*, 480 F. Supp. 429, 203 U.S.P.Q. 656 (C.D. Cal. 1979), rev'd in part, 659 F. 2d 963, 211 U.S.P.Q. 761, 551 PTCJ D-1 (9th Cir. 1981), rev'd, 52 U.S.L.W. 4090 (1984). The *F.E.L. Publications, Ltd., v. Catholic Bishop of Chicago* (N.D. Ill. 1984) jury awarded a composer-publisher of religious music $3,000,000, in actual damages and $1,000,000 in punitive damages for unlawful copying by the Chicago Archdiocese to compensate for business lost. Plaintiff was heard to exclaim "Thank God!" *Meeropol v. Nizer* also found that the future market value of a copyrighted work is an aspect of the potential market. Indeed, "[a]ll publications presumably are operated for profit ..." *Koussevitzky v. Allen, Towne & Heath*, 188 Misc. 479, 483, 68 N.Y.S. 2d 779, 783, aff'd 272 App. Div. 759, 69 N.Y.S. 2d 432 (1st Dept. 1947) (cited in *Rosemont*). However, *Williams & Wilkins Company v. United States* held that while there was merit to the effect on the market of the use, the advancement of medical science and the public interest outweighed these considerations. *Williams & Wilkins* is viewed as having a narrow scope (see Latman, Gorman, & Ginsburg, op. cit.).

20. *House report 94–1476*, op. cit., pp. 68–69.
21. *House report 94–1476*, ibid., pp. 68–69.
22. *House report 94–1476*, ibid., p. 69.
23. *House report 94–1476*, ibid., p. 69.

Chapter 3

1. *House report 94–1476*, ibid., pp. 68–70.
2. While many publishers did sign the agreement, the American Association of University Professors (AAUP), the American Association of Law Schools (AALS) and the American Council of Education (ACE) expressed concern over the guidelines as being too restrictive in a letter

to the Ad Hoc Committee. The Committee replied that "... there is potentially a great deal of educational photocopying beyond that set forth in the guidelines that will clearly be lawful in the future as it has been in the past" (letter, *Chronicle of Higher Education*, October 28, 1978, p. 13).

3. *House report 94–1476*, op. cit., p. 68.
4. *House report 94–1476*, ibid., p. 67.
5. *House report 94–1476*, ibid., p. 67.
6. *House report 94–1476*, ibid., p. 69.
7. *House report 94–1476*, ibid., p. 69.
8. Finkelstein, H. Copyright problems on campus. *The College Counsel*, *6*(1), 203–219.
9. Two discussions on faculty-produced works are (1) Carnahan, W. (1972), Copyright in our realm of learning, *The College Counsel*, *71*(1), 421–447, including work-for-hire aspects; and (2) Zirkel, P. (1975), Copyright law in higher education: Individuals, institutions, and innovations, *Journal of College and University Law*, *2*, 342–354, which discusses various aspects of authorship and use in higher education under the 1976 Copyright Act.
10. See Remer, D. (1982), *Legal care for your software*, Berkeley, CA: Nolo Press; Chapter 6 on work-for-hire agreements in software authorship; and Poking, K., & Meranus, L. (1981), *Law and the writer*, New York: Law-Arts Publishers (on print materials).
11. See *Sherill v. Grieves*, 57 Washington Law Rep. 286, 290 Sup. Ct. D.C. (1929); and *Williams v. Weisser*, 163 U.S.P.Q. 42 (Cal. Ct. App., June 5, 1969).
12. See note #2, Chapter 3.
13. *House report 94–1476*, op. cit., p. 46. See also Sturdevant (Talab), R. (1980), *Print materials in higher education: Selected issues, resulting changes, and "fair use" in the 1976 Copyright Act*, unpublished doctoral dissertation, University of Southern California, for a discussion of materials use in higher education.
14. Letter, *Chronicle of Higher Education*, op. cit., p. 13.

Chapter 4

1. Goldstein, J. (1979). *The performance of copyrighted music: Questions and answers*. New York: Broadcast Music. See also: Erickson, J., Hearn, E., & Halloran, M. (1983), *Musician's guide to copyright* (rev. ed.), New York: Charles Scribner's Sons.
2. Goldstein, ibid., p. 3.
3. *House report 94–1476*, op. cit., p. 71.
4. Taubman, J. (1980). *In tune with the music business* (p. 134). New York: Law-Arts Publishers.
5. Magarrell, J. Harvard University sued for copyright infringement. *The Chronicle of Higher Education*, March 19, 1978, p. 3.
6. *F.E.L. Publications, Ltd., v. Catholic Bishop of Chicago*, op. cit.

7. Goldstein, J., op. cit., p. 2.
8. Goldstein, J., ibid., p. 3. See also Wincor, R. (1982), *Rights contracts in the communications media*, New York: Law & Business, for a good discussion of licensing.
9. Magarrell, J., op. cit., p. 3.

Chapter 5

1. Section 101.
2. Cases which illustrate the copyrightability of video games are: *Midway Mfg. Co. v. Artic International*, 685 F. 2d 870 (3rd Cir. 1982), and *Stern Electronics v. Kaufman*, 669 F. 2d 852 (2d Cir. 1982); both of them held that copying an audiovisual display of video games was infringement. *Williams Electronics Inc., v. Artic International*, 685 F. 2d 870 (3rd Cir. 1982), held infringement of audiovisual display and underlying computer program. *Midway Mfg. Co. v. Strohon*, 564 F. Supp. 741, 219 U.S.P.Q. 42 (1983), held that copyright in a computer program for a video game was protectible separately from the copyright in the audiovisual work and copyright protection extended to object code stored in a chip.
3. Section 106(5).
4. The Betamax case did not rule on pay or cable television, organized or informal "tape swapping," tape duplication by groups or corporations, or for use outside the home (such as for use in the schools). Certainly the most controversial case in off-air taping, though with limited precedent, *Universal City Studios, Inc., v. Sony Corporation of America* was the subject of much discussion. Among the books including discussions of Betamax and off-air taping are: (1) Sinofsky, E. (1984), *Off-air videotaping in education; copyright issues, decisions, implications* (pp. 78–88), New York: R.R. Bowker; (2) Clark, C. (1979–1980), *Universal City Studios, Inc., v. Sony Corporation of America*: Application of the fair use doctrine under the United States Copyright Acts of 1909 and 1976, *New England Law Review, 15*, pp. 161–181; (3) Beard, J. (1979–1980), The sale, rental, and reproduction of motion picture videocassettes: Piracy or privilege? *New England Law Review*, pp. 435–484; and (4) Roberts, M. (1980, March), *Disney/Universal v. Sony*: Arguments and conclusions (Special Report), *The Videocassette and CATV Newsletter*.
5. *House report 94–1476*, p. 64.
6. *House report 94–1476*, ibid., p. 64.
7. *Universal City Studios, Inc., v. Sony Corporation of America*. See notes #19, Chapter 2, and #4, Chapter 5. The court discussed librarying, but found it to be insignificant. However, the BOCES case, see note #4, Chapter 2, found that retention of copies was a cause for infringement. The off-air taping guidelines (see Appendix C) prohibit retention of copies.
8. *House report 94–1476*, op. cit., p. 85.
9. *House report 94–1476*, ibid., p. 86.

10. *House report 94-1476*, ibid., p. 86.
11. *House report 94-1476*, ibid., p. 80.
12. *House report 94-1476*, ibid., p. 81.
13. U.S. Congress. House. See Appendix C.
14. See Sinofsky, op. cit., pp. 98–102 for a discussion and pp. 121–125 for a list of producers who are not endorsing the guidelines.
15. Behrens, S., What can teachers tape off-air? *Current*, May 26, 1980, pp. 1+; and Troost, F. (1978, November), Guidelines for off-air taping policy for schools, *Educational and Industrial Television*, pp. 77–79. Both of these articles discuss interim guidelines for off-air taping before the Congressional guidelines were devised.
16. *Encyclopaedia Britannica Educational Corporation v. Crooks.*
17. Wincor, R., op. cit.
18. While Section 110 is the section that pertains to off-air taping in the non-profit institution, the *House report 94-1476*, op. cit., pp. 81–88, explains the stipulations of 110 more clearly. For a discussion of Section 110 and the off-air taping guidelines, see Miller, J.K. (1984), *Using copyrighted videocassettes in classrooms and libraries*, Champaign, IL: Copyright Information Services; and Billings, R.D. (1977), Off-air videorecording, face-to-face teaching, and the 1976 Copyright Act, *Northern Kentucky Law Review, 4*, 225–251.
19. While it could be argued that the limited use of closed circuit could be used to transmit a program to a "cluster or campus," the *House report 94-1476*, op. cit., pp. 80–81, specifically prohibits closed circuit. This is, then, an area of contention.
20. See in J.S. Lawrence & B. Timberg (Eds.) (1980), *Fair Use and free inquiry*, Norwood, NJ: Ablex, for discussions of off-air taping and television research: Mast, G., Film study and copyright law (pp. 71–80); Kellner, D., Television research and fair use (pp. 90–107); Kies, C., The CBS-Vanderbilt litigation: Taping the evening news (pp. 111–119); and Aleinikoff, E., Fair use and broadcasting (pp. 180–191).
21. See Miller, J.K., *The Video/Copyright Seminar 1986* (annual), Copyright Information Services, for a discussion of the application of the Communications Act to satellite off-air taping; and Bender, I. (1985, November), Copyright implications of satellite transmissions, *TLC Guide*, p. 8, for another view. While these views do not necessarily conflict, their discussions point out the essential grayness of satellite off-air taping at present.
22. Stanek, D.J. (1986, March). Videotapes, computer programs, and the library. *Information Technology and Libraries*, pp. 42–54. See also Reed, M.H., & Stanek, D. (1986, February), Library and classroom use of copyrighted videotapes and computer software, *American Libraries*. Cases which have to do with public exhibition of videos, delineating what constitutes a public performance, are *Columbia Pictures Industries, Inc., v. Redd Horne, Inc.*, 749 F. 2d 154 (3d Cir. 1984), which dealt with in-store viewing of rented tapes; and *Columbia Pictures Industries, Inc., v. Aveco, Inc.*, 612 F. Supp. 315 (M.D. Pa. 1985), which dealt with (1) renting viewing rooms and cassettes separately and (2) customer-operated videocassette players. Both were considered similar and infringements.

23. See in J.S. Lawrence & B. Timberg (1980): Douglass, J., Seeking copyright clearances for an audiovisual center (pp. 121–125); and Miller, J., The duplication of audiovisual materials for libraries (pp. 127–128).

Chapter 6

1. Tapper, C. (1982). *Computer law* (2nd ed.). New York: Longman Group, Limited. See also CONTU, *Final report*, op. cit., p. 23. See also: objections to the copyrightability of software in Koenig, C.F. (1980), Software copyright: The conflict within CONTU, *Bulletin of the Copyright Society of the U.S.A.*, *27*, 340–378. Court cases have firmly established the copyrightability of software. See *Apple Computer, Inc. v. Franklin Computer Corporation*, 545 F. Supp. 812 (E.D. Pa. 1982), rev'd 714 F. 2d 1240 (3d Cir. 1983), which confirms "categorical" copyrightability of computer programs, "... a computer program is a 'work of authorship' subject to copyright ..." *Tandy Corporation v. Personal MicroComputers, Inc.*, 524 F. Supp. 171 (N.D. Cal. 1981), copyrightability of ROM; *Williams Electronics, Inc., v. Artic International, Inc.*, chip duplication as "copy" which Congress clearly intended to protect; and *Apple Computer, Inc., v. Formula International, Inc.*, 725 F. 2d 521 (9th Cir. 1984), in which Apple was granted a preliminary injunction against Formula's selling "Pineapples" that included copies of Apple's "autostart" ROMs. See Latman, Gorman, & Ginsburg, op. cit., pp. 137–138 for a discussion.
2. CONTU, *Final report*, op. cit., p. 26.
3. CONTU, *Final report*, ibid., p. 38.
4. *House report 94-1476*, op. cit., p. 116.
5. *P.L. 96-517, Copyright law amendment for computer programs* (94 Stat. 3028–29), December 12, 1980. Another amendment allowed "mask works" to be copyrighted. *P.L. 98-620, The Semiconductor Chip Protection Act of 1984*, January 23, 1984, provided copyright protection for a new class of writings—mask works. This protection lasts for 10 years from the effective date of registration or from the date of the first commercial exploitation, whichever comes first. For a discussion of this act, see Miller, P., Computer software and related technology, in M. Goldberg (Ed.), *Current developments in copyright law 1985* (pp. 369–422), New York: Practicing Law Institute.
6. Brooks, D. (1984–1985). Acquisition and exploitation of custom software. In M. Goldberg (Ed.), *Computer software 1984; protection and marketing* (Vols. 1–2, pp. 659–833; p. 765). New York: Practicing Law Institute.
7. Baumgarten, J. (1984). Copyright and computer software, databases and chip technology (including summary of recent development). In M. Goldberg, op. cit. (Vol. 1, pp. 27–28); discusses award possibilities according to whether registration is made (1) before the infringing action or (2) after the infringing action has commenced, as well as other aspects of registration. Peters, M. (1985). Copyright formalities: Notice, deposit, and registration. In M. Goldberg, ibid. (Vol. 1, pp. 149–174); also has a good discussion of registration, infringement, and remedies.

8. Finkel, L. (1985, April/May). Editorial opinion. *Computer-Using Educators*, p. 3.
9. The International Council for Computers in Education (ICCE) has pioneered the need for backups, multiple-copy discounts, and other aspects of software use. See Finkel, L., *Computer-Using Educators* position paper on commercial software pricing policies, *The Computing Teacher*, 8(6), 53, for the first position paper; and ICCE (1983, September), ICCE policy statement on network and multiple-machine software, *The Computing Teacher*, pp. 18–22, for the second position paper. A committee has been reconvened for the purpose of drawing up a third position paper. See: *The Computing Teacher* (1985, March). See also Finkel, L., & Wagner, S. (1983, March), Software copyright protection policies, *Classroom Computer News*, p. 102, for the history of CUE's efforts; Talab, R.S. (1984, January), The problem of copying computer programs without breaking the law, *Instructional Innovator*, pp. 36–37, for discussion of policy efforts by various organizations; and Talab, R.S. (1985, February/March), Look both ways before copying, *TechTrends*, for the status of software copyright.
10. Section 103.
11. Recent decisions which confirm the copyrightability of databases and compilations are: *Financial Information, Inc., v. Moody's Investors Service, Inc.*, 751 F. 2d 501 (2d Cir. 1984); *Dow Jones & Co., Inc., v. Board of Trade of the City of Chicago*, 546 F. Supp. 113, 217 U.S.P.Q. 901 (1982); *National Business Lists, Inc., v. Dun & Bradstreet, Inc.*, 552 F. Supp. 89, 215 U.S.P.Q. 595 (1982); *Rand McNally & Co. v. Fleet Management Systems*, 591 F. Supp. 726 (N.D. Ill. 1983).
12. *House report 94–1476*, op. cit., p. 54.
13. Baumgarten, J. (1984). Copyright and computer software (including databases and chip technology). In Goldberg, M., op. cit. (Vol. 1, p. 57).
14. Downloading and piracy. (1984, May). *Download*, pp. 13–14. See also: Electronic distribution of software. (1985, January). *Copyright Management*, pp. 4–5.
15. Jansen, A. (1984, January). Problems and challenges of downloading for database producers. *The Electronic Library*, pp. 41–49. See also: Warrick, T. (1984, July), Large databases, small computers and fast modems ... an attorney looks at the legal ramifications of downloading, *Online*, pp. 58–70; Wolfe, M. (1982, July), Copyright and machine readable databases, *Online*, pp. 52–55; and Rosenberg, V. (1984, October 30), Downloading in the 1990's, *Online 1984 Proceedings* (no page numbers).
16. Jansen, A., ibid., p. 42.
17. Jansen, A., ibid., p. 45.
18. Baumgarten, J. (1984). Primer of the principles of international copyright. In K. Steele (Ed.), *Electronic information publishing; old issues in a new industry* (pp. 241–264). New York: Practicing Law Institute.
19. *House report 94–1476*, op. cit., p. 61. See *Rand McNally & Co. v. Fleet Management Systems*, 591 F. Supp. 726 (N.D. Ill. 1983); held that the copyright law protects the "industrious compilation of facts ... even where the facts compiled are collected from public sources."

20. Baumgarten, J., op. cit., p. 66.
21. Baumgarten, J., ibid., p. 66.
22. Squires, R. (1979). Copyright and computer-readable databases. In J. Bush & D. Dreyfuss (Eds.), *Copyright litigation* (p. 235). New York: Practicing Law Institute.
23. Squires, ibid., p. 235.
24. INSPEC. Downloading from the INSPEC database—a statement of policy. *INSPEC Matters*, No. 38. pp. 1–2.
25. Latman, Gorman, & Ginsburg, op. cit., p. 131.
26. Latman, Gorman, & Ginsburg, ibid., p. 131.
27. For example, perusal of the INSPEC, DIALOG, Excerpta Medica, Chemical Abstracts, and BIOSIS policies indicates basic agreement on database downloading terms.
28. Baumgarten, J. (1984). Current issues concerning copyright protection of software and databases internationally. In M. Goldberg, op. cit. (Vol. 1, p. 65).
29. *Financial Information, Inc., v. Moody's Investors Service, Inc.*, 751 F. 2d 501 (2d Cir. 1984).
30. See *National Business Lists, Inc., v. Dun and Bradstreet, Inc.*, 552 F. Supp. 89, 215 U.S.P.Q. 595 (1982); held that "[t]he public interest in dissemination becomes progressively stronger as we move along the spectrum from fancy to fact." *New York Times Co. v. Roxbury Data Interface, Inc.*, 434 F. Supp. 217, 194 U.S.P.Q. 371 (D. NJ. 1977), held that the use by the defendant to prepare a personal name index to plaintiff's work was fair use.
31. Latman, Gorman, & Ginsburg, op. cit., p. 131.
32. CONTU, *Final report*, op. cit., p. 40.
33. CONTU, *Final report*, ibid., p. 40.
34. "The example of a copyrighted work placed in a computer memory solely to facilitate an individual's scholarly research has been cited as a possible fair use. The Commission agrees that such a use, restricted to individual research, should be considered fair." CONTU, *Final report*, op. cit., p. 40. "Only if information of a substantial amount were extracted and duplicated for redistribution would serious problems exist ..." Latman, Gorman, & Ginsburg, op. cit., p. 134. In all cases, the records should then be destroyed.
35. "Computer Software Piracy and Counterfeiting Amendments of 1984" (H.R. 4646). Cited in Boorstyn, N. (1984), Copyright protection and computer software. In M. Goldberg, op. cit. (Vol. 2, pp. 389–406, p. 406).
36. Bell, T. Copying computer software for educational purposes: Is it allowed? *Personal Computing*, Nov. 1983, pp. 236–242.
37. Micropro sued United Computer for infringement of a program by making multiple copies for company use. See: Lotus charges software piracy in test case (1984, February), *Copyright Management*, pp. 5–6, in which Lotus Development Corporation filed suit against Rixon, a subsidiary of Sangamo Western, distributing 13 unauthorized copies of Lotus 1-2-3 to its branch offices. This was the first major suit by a software developer against a customer that distributed copied software for internal use. See also: Anti-software piracy fund formed (1984, November), *Copyright*

Management, p. 4. Ashton Tate, Lotus, Sorcum and Microsoft have formed a "software piracy fund" to be used in combating illegal copying. They also hope to influence copyright legislation and work closely with ADAPSO (The Association of Data Processing Service Organizations).

Chapter 7

1. *House report 94-1476*, op. cit., p. 122.
2. Ibid.
3. Polking, K., & Meranus, L. *Law and the writer* (p. 52). Cincinnati, OH: Writer's Digest Books.
4. Dannay, R. (1985). In M. Goldberg (Ed.), *Current developments in copyright law 1985* (pp. 171-210). New York: Practicing Law Institute.
5. Peters, M. (1985). Copyright formalities: Notice, deposit, and registration. In M. Goldberg, op. cit., (pp. 149-170). Cited in this article are two pertinent cases illustrating the need for registration: (1) *International Trade Management, Inc., v. U.S.*, 553 F. Supp. 402 (U.S. Ct. Cl. 1982); and (2) *Proulx v. Hennepin Technical Centers School District No. 287*, CCH Copr. L. Rep. Section 25, 389 (D. Minn. Dec. 31, 1981). See also Erickson, J., Hearn, E., & Halloran, M. (1983). *Musician's guide to copyright* (rev. ed., p. 36). New York: Charles Scribner's Sons.
6. Peters, M., ibid., p. 162.
7. Halloran, M., & Tulchin, J. (1984). In N. Beil (Ed.), *The writer's legal and business guide* (pp. 52-64). New York: Arco Publishing.

Chapter 8

1. *House report 94-1476*, op. cit., p. 67.
2. Section 504(c).
3. Carnahan, W., op. cit., p. 445.
4. J. Douglass has works on this subject: (1) Copyright as it affects instructional development (1974, December), *Audiovisual Instruction*, pp. 37-38; and (2) Seeking copyright clearances for an audiovisual center (1980), in J. Lawrence & B. Timberg (Eds.), *Fair use and free inquiry; copyright law and the new media* (pp. 121-126), Norwood, NJ: Ablex Pub. Corp. See also Mucklow, E. (1977, March), Steps for resolving the duplication dilemma, *Community and Junior College Journal*, pp. 14-17.
5. American Association of Publishers/Authors League. (1978). *A guide to permissions*. New York: American Association of Publishers/Author's League.
6. *House report 94-1476*, op. cit., p. 14.
7. Gross, L., & Millington, W. (1978, February). Coping with the new copyright law. *Change Magazine*, pp. 24-26.

Chapter 9

1. Lucker, J.K. (1983). Copyright and libraries—a librarian's perspective. In J. Baumgarten & A. Latman (Eds.), *Corporate copyright and information practices* (p. 152). New York: Practicing Law Institute.
2. Copyright Office, Library of Congress. (1983, January). *Report of the Register of Copyrights: Library reproduction of copyrighted works* (17 U.S.C. 108) (p. viii). Washington, DC: U.S. Government Printing Office. (Herein after referred to as *Register's report*.)
3. American Library Association. (1983, January). *Comments of the American Library Association on the Report of the Register of Copyrights to Congress: Library reproduction of copyrighted works (17 U.S.C. 108)*. Chicago: ALA.
4. ALA, ibid.
5. Latman, A., & Gorman, R. (1985). Copyright for the eighties (2nd ed., p. 522). Charlottesville, VA: Michie/Bobbs-Merrill. This is indicated in the *Register's report* (p. 195).
6. Two sources that indicate this belief are: (1) Martell, C. (1979, July). Copyright—one year later: A symposium. *Journal of Academic Librarianship*, 5(3), 124-131; (2) Byrd, G. (1981, April). Copyright compliance in health sciences libraries: A status report two after the implementation of P.L. 94-553. *Bulletin of the Medical Library Association*, 69(2), 224-230.
7. Lucker, J.K., op. cit., p. 157.
8. *Register's report*, op. cit., p. 359.
9. Section 108(a)(1).
10. Section 108(a)(2).
11. Section 108 (a)(3).
12. Section 108(d).
13. Section 108(d)(1).
14. Section 108(d)(1).
15. Section 108 (d)(2).
16. Section 108(g)(1).
17. Section 108(g)(2).
18. Section 108(g)(2).
19. 37 C.F.R. Section 201, 14, 1984.
20. See: *Register's report*, op. cit., p. 127, in which the *Senate report no. 473* is quoted at p. 70.
21. *Register's report*, ibid., p. 127.
22. Section 108 (g)(1).
23. Section 108(e)(2). "Nothing in this section in any way affects the right of fair use as provided by Section 107."
24. Guidelines for educational uses of music, Section (A)(1).
25. Section 108(c).
26. Section 108(b).
27. Section 108(c).
28. Section 108 (a)(1) and (d)(2).
29. Section 108(g)(1).

30. Section 108(h).
31. CONTU, op. cit., p. 5.
32. *Conference report, House report 94-1733* (Comm. of Conference) (1976, September 29, 94th Congress on S.22) (pp. 71–73).
33. American Library Association. (1977). *Librarian's copyright kit.* Chicago: ALA.
34. Byrd, G., op. cit., p. 226.
35. Martell, C. Copyright and reserve operations—an interpretation. *College and Research Libraries News*, No. 1:1, pp. 1–2.
36. *Register's report*, op. cit., p. 2.
37. Heller, J., & Wiant, S.K. (1984). *Copyright handbook* (AALL Publications Series) (p. 23). Littleton, CO: Fred B. Rothman & Co.
38. *House report 94-1476*, op. cit., pp. 72–74.
39. *Register's report*, op. cit., p. 133.
40. *Register's report*, ibid., p. 136.
41. *Register's report*, ibid., p. 78.
42. *Register's report*, ibid., p. 156.
43. *Register's report*, ibid., p. 157.
44. *Register's report*, ibid., p. 78.
45. *Register's report*, ibid., p. 79.
46. *Register's report*, ibid., p. 78.
47. *House report 94-1476*, op. cit., p. 75.
48. *House report 94-1476*, ibid., p. 75.
49. Lucker, J.K., op. cit., pp. 149–151.
50. Copyright Office, Library of Congress. (1983, March). Warnings of copyright for use by libraries and archives. *Circular R 96* (Section 201.14). Washington, DC: U.S. Government Printing Office.
51. *Register's report*, op. cit., p. 108.
52. *Register's report*, ibid., p. 110; American Library Association (1982), *Model policy concerning college and university photocopying for classroom, research, and library reserve use*, Chicago: ALA; and Heller, J., & Wiant, S.K. (1984), *Copyright handbook* (American Association of Law Libraries—AALL Series) (p. 29), Littleton, CO: Fred B. Rothman & Co.
53. *Register's report*, op. cit., p. 110.
54. This position was originally taken by the American Association of Publishers (AAP) in *Photocopying by academic, public, and non-profit research libraries* (1978), New York: AAP.
55. Snyder cited a study in 1978 in which 15 out of 27 institutions did not restrict repeated use.
56. Stedman, J. (1978), Academic library reserves, photocopying and the copyright law, *College and Research Library News*, 9:263, 266; Nimmer, M. (1978), *3 Nimmer on copyright* (pp. 13–63); see Snyder's article for a thorough examination of reserve room practices in Snyder, F., Copyright and the library reserve room, *Law Library Journal*, 73, 702–714. See notes #20–22 for a discussion of other photocopying practice restrictions.
57. *House report 94-1476*, op. cit., p. 68.
58. *Register's report*, op. cit., p. 72.
59. *Register's report*, ibid., p. 72.

60. Snyder, F., op. cit., p. 713.
61. Heller & Wiant, op. cit., p. 28.
62. ALA, op. cit., Ch. 4, note 10, at 4–6.
63. *Register's report*, op. cit., p. 247.
64. Heller & Wiant, op. cit., p. 25.
65. *House report 94–1476*, op. cit., p. 72.
66. Copyright Clearance Center, Inc., 21 Congress Street, Salem, MA 01970; (617) 744-3350. See also section on Copyright Clearance Center and *The Bowker annual of library and book trade information* (27th ed.) (1982), New York: R.R. Bowker, for a complete listing of the CCC's services and programs.
67. The *MLA Bulletin* published by the Medical Library Association regularly publishes information on this practice.

Chapter 10

1. Stanek, D.J. (1986, March). Videotapes, computer programs, and the library. *Information Technology and Libraries*, pp. 42–54.
2. Letter from Burton H. Hanft to Jerome K. Miller. (1983, August 12). Cited in Stanek, D.J., ibid.
3. U.S. Congress, House, Judiciary Committee. (1976). *Report No. 94–1476* (p. 159) (94th Congress, 2nd Session).
4. Letter to the author. (1985, August 16). MGM/UA.
5. See Stanek, D.J., op. cit.; and Hutchins, M.R., & Stanek, D.J. (1986, February), Library and classroom use of copyrighted videotapes and computer software, *American Libraries*. For further discussion of exhibition, see: *Columbia Pictures Industries, Inc., v. Redd Horne, Inc.,* 749 F. 2d 154 (3d Cir. 1984), in which a video rental store offered an "in-store rental" service; and *Columbia Pictures Industries, Inc., v. Aveco, Inc.*, 612 F. Supp. 315 (M.D. Pa. 1985), in which the Nickelodeon Video Showcase operated similarly to Maxwell's, except that (1) it rented viewing rooms and cassettes separately, (2) Nickelodeon customers operated the videocassette players on their own, and (3) Nickelodeon yielded physical possession of the videotapes to customers.
6. Bell, T. (1983, November). Copying computer software for educational purposes: Is it allowed? *Personal Computing* pp. 236–242. See also Talab, R. (1984, Summer), Copyright, microcomputer software, and the library media center. *School Library Media Quarterly*, pp. 285–288.
7. Pattie, K. (1985, October). Copyright abuse: No need for lawsuits. *Tech-Trends*, pp. 40 + .
8. Personal communication of Kenton Pattie to the author (1985, November).
9. International Council on Computers in Education (ICCE). (1983, July 1). *ICCE policy statement on network and multiple machine software.* (See Appendix D.)
10. San Diego County Instructional Resource Center. (1982, December). Request for examination of copyrighted courseware. *The Computing Teacher*, p. 41.

11. *1986 ICCE policy statement on software copyright.* See also Finkel, L. (1985, March). Software copyright interpretation. *The Computing Teacher*, p. 10.
12. OTA Intellectual Property Rights Questionnaire. (1985, March). *The Computing Teacher*, p. 11. See also The new agenda on intellectual property rights, *TechTrends*, May/June, 1986, pp. 3-6, for a discussion of the results of this study.
13. *Screen Gems—Columbia Music, Inc., v. Mack-fi Records*, F. Supp. at 791, 792 (as cited by *Universal City Studios*, 480 F. Supp. at 460). A discussion of contributory infringement is in Latman and Gorman's *Copyright in the eighties*, op. cit., pp. 532–533.

CHART A
SIMPLIFIED GUIDELINES FOR PRINT MATERIALS AND COMPUTER SOFTWARE*
in Nonprofit Educational Institutions

Material	Fiction Nonfiction Textbooks Theses	Stories Essays Anthologies Encyclopedias	Poetry	Periodicals	Cartoons Charts Pictures	Lectures Sermons Speeches	Computer Software and Documentation
Instructor's Copy	1 chapter	1 story or essay	1 article	1 article	1 per book or issue	1 per book or issue	1 archival copy[1]
Multiple Copies	1,000-word excerpt or 10%	2,500-word excerpt or story	250-word excerpt or poem	2,500-word excerpt or essay	Same as above	Same as above	? small excerpts only of documentation[2]
Cumulative Use Per Class Per Term	2	2-3	2	3	2-3	2-3	?

*The law permits a combination of nine instances of any of the above usages per course per term; free use may be made of newspapers—no limit; workbooks, manuals, standardized tests, study guides, etc., are prohibited.

[1] The same rules apply to the software itself.
[2] Multiple copies may only be made by lease or purchase agreement.

CHART B
SIMPLIFIED LIBRARY DUPLICATING GUIDELINES

	Purpose	Books	Periodicals	Musical Works	Cartoons Charts Diagrams Graphics Pictorial Works	Audiovisual News Programs	Computer Software and documentation
One Copy	archival reproduction	yes	yes	yes	yes	yes	yes
	replacement of damaged, stolen or lost copy[1]	yes	yes	yes	yes	yes	? yes[2]
	out-of-print work[1]	yes	yes	yes	yes	N/A	? yes
	interlibrary loan	1 chapter or 10%	1 per issue	10%	1 per book or issue	1 per book or issue	yes
	interlibrary loan	same as above	5 per calendar year for past 5 years	no guidelines	no guidelines	no guidelines	no guidelines
Multiple Copies	unsupervised photocopiers	The library is not responsible as long as copyright warning is posted.					
	teacher and student copies	See Simplified Guidelines for Print Materials, Chart A.					
	reserve desk	One copy is legal; more copies than that depends on usage and subscription policies. (See Chapter Three, Reserve Room Photocopying.)					

[1]If unavailable at a fair price.
[2]Only a damaged copy may be replaced by an archival copy. The copy is not to be used to extend the life of the original.

CHART C
SIMPLIFIED GUIDELINES FOR MOTION PICTURE AND TELEVISION OFF-AIR TAPING

Medium	PBS Programs Cleared for Taping[2]	Commercial Television Programs[5]	Television Audiovisual News Programs[3]	Subscription Television Programs	Motion Pictures
Live transmission to classroom	yes	yes	yes	no	no
Teacher's copy for limited period classroom use[1]	yes	yes	no[4]	no	fair use amount; in film or stills

[1]Ten days for a once-only use in instructional activities with a once-only repetition for reinforcement purposes; copy may be held up to 45 days before erasure. (See Appendix C.)

[2]PBS Video has a newsletter on programs available, as does the Television Licensing Center.

[3]Does not include magazine format or documentary news programs.

[4]May be retained by a library or archive open to the public for purposes of research, criticism, or comment.

[5]"...It appears that satellite reception of *broadcast* television programs [simultaneously rebroadcast—ABC, CBS, NBC affiliates which require no fee, for example] may be taped off-air.*

*Bender, I. (1985, November). Copyright implications of satellite transmissions. *TLC Guide*, p. 8.

Part V
Appendices

Appendix A
Agreement on Guidelines for Classroom Copying in Not-for-Profit Educational Institutions

With Respect to Books and Periodicals

The purpose of the following guidelines is to state the minimum and not the maximum standards of educational fair use under Section 107 of H.R. 2223. The parties agree that the conditions determining the extent of permissible copying for educational purposes may change in the future; that certain types of copying permitted under these guidelines may not be permissible in the future; and conversely that in the future other types of copying not permitted under these guidelines may be permissible under revised guidelines. Moreover, the following statement of guidelines is not intended to limit the types of copying permitted under the standards of fair use under judicial decision and which are stated in Section 107 of the Copyright Revision Bill. There may be instances in which copying which does not fall within the guidelines stated below may nonetheless be permitted under the criteria of fair use.

GUIDELINES

I. Single Copying for Teachers

A single copy may be made of any of the following by or for a teacher at his or her individual request for his or her scholarly research or use in teaching or preparation to teach a class:

A. A chapter from a book.

B. An article from a periodical or newspaper.

C. A short story, short essay or short poem, whether or not from a collective work.

D. A chart, graph, diagram, drawing, cartoon or picture from a book, periodical, or newspaper.

II. Multiple Copies for Classroom Use

Multiple copies (not to exceed in any event more than one copy per pupil in a course) may be made by or for the teacher giving the course for classroom use or discussion; provided that:

A. The copying meeting the tests of brevity and spontaneity as defined below.

B. The copying meets the cumulative effect test as defined below.

C. Each copy includes a notice of copyright.

Definitions

  Brevity

   (i) Poetry: (a) A complete poem is less than 250 words and if printed on not more than two pages, or (b) from a longer poem, an excerpt of not more than 250 words.

  (ii) Prose: (a) Either a complete article, story or essay of less than 2,500 words, or (b) an excerpt from any prose work of not more than 1,000 words or 10 percent of the work, whichever is less, but in any event a minimum of 500 words.

(Each of the numerical limits stated in "i" and "ii" above may be expanded to permit the completion of an unfinished line of a poem or of an unfinished prose paragraph.)

 (iii) Illustration: one chart, graph, diagram, drawing, cartoon or picture per book or periodical issue.

 (iv) "Special" works: Certain works in poetry, prose or in "poetic prose" which often combine language with illustrations and which are intended sometimes for children and at other times for a more general audience fall short of 2,500 words in their entirety. Paragraph "ii" above notwithstanding such "special works" may not be reproduced in their entirety; however, an excerpt comprising not more than two of the published pages of such special work and containing not more than 10 percent of the words found in the text thereof, may be reproduced.

Spontaneity
  (i) The copying is at the instance and inspiration of the individual teacher, and
  (ii) the inspiration and decision to use the work and the moment of its use for maximum teaching effectiveness are so close in time that it would be unreasonable to expect a timely reply to a request for permission.

Cumulative Effect
  (i) The copying of the material is for only one course in the school in which the copies are made.
  (ii) Not more than one short poem, article, story, essay or two excerpts may be copied from the same author, not more than three from the same collective work or periodical volume during one class term.
  (iii) There shall not be more than nine instances of such multiple copying for one course during one class term. The limitations stated in "ii" and "iii" above shall not apply to current news periodicals and newspapers and current news sections of other periodicals.

III. Prohibitions as to I and II Above

Notwithstanding any of the above, the following shall be prohibited:

A. Copying shall not be used to create or to replace or substitute for anthologies, compilations or collective works. Such replacement or substitution may occur whether copies of various works or excerpts therefrom are accumulated or reproduced and used separately.

B. There shall be no copying from works intended to be "consumable" in the course of study or of teaching. These include workbooks, exercises, standardized tests and test booklets and answer sheets and like consumable material.

C. Copying shall not:
  a. substitute for the purchase of books, publishers' reprints or periodicals;
  b. be directed by higher authority;
  c. be repeated with respect to the same item by the same teacher from term to term;
  d. no charge shall be made to the student beyond the actual cost of the photocopying.

Appendix B
Guidelines for
Educational Use of Music

The purpose of the following guidelines is to state the minimum and not the maximum standards of educational fair use under Section 107 of HR 2223. The parties agree that the conditions determining the extent of permissible copying for educational purposes may change in the future; that certain types of copying permitted under these guidelines may not be permissible in the future, and conversely that in the future other types of copying not permitted under these guidelines may be permissible under revised guidelines.

Moreover, the following statement of guidelines is not intended to limit the types of copying permitted under the standards of fair use under judicial decision and which are stated in Section 107 of the Copyright Revision Bill. There may be instances in which copying which does not fall within the guidelines stated below may nonetheless be permitted under the criteria of fair use.

A. Permissible Uses

    1. Emergency copying to replace purchased copies which for any reason are not available for an imminent performance provided purchased replacement copies shall be substitutes in due course.

    2. (a) For academic purposes other than performance, single or multiple copies of excerpts of works may be made, provided that the excerpts do not comprise a part of the whole which would constitute a performable unit such as a selection, movement, or aria, but in no case more than 10 percent of the whole work. The number of copies shall not exceed one copy per pupil.*

    (b) For academic purposes other than performance, a single

122

copy of an entire performable unit such as a section, movement, or aria, that is, (1) confirmed by the copyright proprietor to be out of print or (2) unavailable except in a larger work, may be made by or for a teacher solely for the purpose of his or her scholarly research or in preparation to teach a class.

3. Printed copies which have been purchased may be edited or simplified provided that the fundamental character of the work is not distorted or the lyrics, if any, altered or lyrics added if none exist.

4. A single copy of recordings of performances by students may be made for evaluation or rehearsal purposes and may be retained by the educational institution or individual teacher.

5. A single copy of a sound recording (such as a tape, disc or cassette) of copyrighted music may be made from sound recordings owned by an educational institution or an individual teacher. (This pertains only to the copyright of the music itself and not to any copyright which may exist in the sound recording.)

B. Prohibitions

1. Copying to create or replace or substitute for anthologies, compilations, or collective works.

2. Copying from works intended to be "consumable" in the course of study or of teaching, such as workbooks, exercises, standardized tests and answer sheets and like material.

3. Copying for the purpose of performance, except as in A(1) above.

4. Copying for the purpose of substituting for the purchase of music, except as in A(1) and A(2) above.

5. Copying without inclusion of the copyright notice which appears on the printed copy.

Section 2a as amended in the Congressional Record, *September 22, 1976, p. 31980.*

Appendix C
Guidelines for Off-Air Recording of Broadcast Programming for Educational Purposes

In accordance with what we believe was (the) intent, the Negotiating Committee has limited its discussion to nonprofit educational institutions and to television programs broadcast for reception by the general public without charge. Within the guidelines, the Negotiating Committee does not intend that off-air recordings by teachers under fair use be permitted to be intentionally substituted in the school curriculum for a standard practice of purchase or license of the same educational material by the institution concerned.

1. The guidelines were developed to apply only to off-air recordings by non-profit educational institutions.

2. A broadcast program may be recorded off-air simultaneously with broadcast transmission (including simultaneous cable retransmission) and retained by a non-profit educational institution for a period not to exceed the first forty-five (45) consecutive calendar days after date of recording. Upon conclusion of such retention period, all off-air recordings must be erased or destroyed immediately. "Broadcast programs" are television programs transmitted by television stations for reception by the general public without charge.

3. Off-air recordings may be used once by individual teachers in the course of relevant teaching activities, and repeated once only when instructional reinforcement is necessary, in classrooms and similar places devoted to instruction within a single building, cluster or campus, as well as in the homes of students

receiving formalized home instruction, during the first ten (10) consecutive school days in the forty-five (45) day calendar day retention period.

4. Off-air recordings may be made only at the request of and used by individual teachers, and may not be regularly recorded in anticipation of requests. No broadcast program may be recorded off-air more than once at the request of the same teacher, regardless of the number of times the program may be broadcast.

5. A limited number of copies may be reproduced from each off-air recording to meet the legitimate needs of teachers under these guidelines. Each such additional copy shall be subject to all provisions governing the original recording.

6. After the first ten (10) consecutive school days, off-air recordings may be used up to the end of the forty-five (45) calendar day retention period only for teacher evaluation purposes, i.e., to determine whether or not to include the broadcast program in the teaching curriculum, and may not be used in the recording institution for student exhibition or any other non-evaluation purpose without authorization.

7. Off-air recordings need not be used in their entirety, but the recorded programs may not be altered from their original content. Off-air recordings may not be physically or electronically combined or merged to constitute teaching anthologies or compilations.

8. All copies of off-air recordings must include the copyright notice on the broadcast program as recorded.

9. Educational institutions are expected to establish appropriate control procedures to maintain the integrity of these guidelines.

Appendix D
ICCE Policy Statement on Network and Multiple Machine Software

Just as there has been shared responsibility in the development of this policy, so should there be shared responsibility for resolution of the problems inherent in providing and securing good educational software. Educators have a valid need for quality software and reasonable prices. Hardware developers and or vendors also must share in the effort to enable educators to make maximum cost-effective use of that equipment. Software authors, developers and vendors are entitled to a fair return on their investment.

Educators' Responsibilities

Educators need to face the legal and ethical issues involved in copyright laws and publisher license agreements and must accept the responsibility for enforcing adherence to these laws and agreements. Budget constraints do not excuse illegal use of software.

Educators should be prepared to provide software developers or their agents with a district-level approved written policy statement including as a minimum:

1. A clear requirement that copyright laws and publisher license agreements be observed;
2. A statement making teachers who use school equipment responsible for taking all reasonable precautions to prevent copying or the use of unauthorized copies on school equipment;
3. An explanation of the steps taken to prevent unauthorized copying or the use of unauthorized copies on school equipment;

4. A designation of who is authorized to sign software license agreements for the school (or district);
5. A designation at the school site level of who is responsible for enforcing the terms of the district policy and terms of licensing agreements;
6. A statement indicating teacher responsibility for educating students about the legal, ethical and practical problems caused by illegal use of software.

Hardware Vendors' Responsibilities

Hardware vendors should assist educators in making maximum cost effective use of the hardware and help in enforcing software copyright laws and license agreements. They should as a minimum:

1. Make efforts to see that illegal copies of programs are not being distributed by their employees and agents;

2. Work cooperatively with interested software developers to provide an encryption process which avoids inflexibility but discourages theft.

Software Developers'/Vendors' Responsibilities

Software developers and their agents can share responsibility for helping educators observe copyright laws and publishers' license agreements by developing sales and pricing policies. Software developers and vendors should as a minimum:

1. Provide for all software a back-up copy to be used for archival purposes, to be included with every purchase;
2. Provide for on-approval purchases to allow schools to preview the software to ensure that it meets the needs and expectations of the educational institution. Additionally, software developers are encouraged to provide regional or area centers with software for demonstration purposes. The ICCE encourages educators to develop regional centers for this purpose;
3. Work in cooperation with hardware vendors to provide an encryption process which avoids inflexibility but discourages theft;
4. Provide for, and note in advertisements, multiple-copy pricing for school sites with several machines and recognize that multiple copies do not necessarily call for multiple documentation;

5. Provide for, and note in advertisements, network-compatible versions of software with pricing structures that recognize the extra costs of development to secure compatibility and recognize the buyer's need for only a single copy of the software.

The Board of Directors of The International Council for Computers in Education approved this policy statement, with attachments, June 5, 1983. The committee that drafted this policy included: Jenny Better, Director of Curriculum, Cupertino Union Elementary District; LeRoy Finkel, San Mateo County Office of Education; Pennie Gallant, Apple Computer, Inc.; John Hazelwood/Jeffrey Armstrong, Corvus Systems, Inc.; Marion B. Kenworthy, Saratoga High School; Richard R. Monnard, Addison-Wesley Publishing Co.; Henry Vigil/Cliff Godwin, Cybertronics International; and William Wagner, Santa Clara County Office of Education.

ATTACHMENT 1
Suggested District Policy on Software Copyright

It is the intent of _____ to adhere to the provisions of copyright laws in the area of microcomputer programs. Though there continues to be controversy regarding interpretation of those copyright laws, the following procedures represent a sincere effort to operate legally. We recognize that computer software piracy is a major problem for the industry and that violations of computer copyright laws contribute to higher costs and greater efforts to prevent copies and or lessen incentives for the development of good educational software. All of these results are detrimental to the development of effective educational uses of microcomputers. Therefore, in an effort to discourage violation of copyright laws and to prevent such illegal activities:

1. The ethical and practical problems caused by software piracy will be taught in all schools in the District.
2. District employees will be expected to adhere to the provisions of Public Law 96-517, Section 7(b) which amends Section 117 of Title 17 of the United States Code to allow for the making of a back-up copy of computer programs. This states that "...it is not an infringement for the owner of a copy of a computer program to make or authorize the making of another copy or adaptation of that computer program provided:
   a. that such a new copy or adaptation is created as an essential step in the utilization of the computer program in conjunction with a machine and that it is used in no other manner, or

    b. that such a new copy and adaptation is for archival purposes only and that all archival copies are destroyed in the event that continued possession of the computer program should cease to be rightful."

3. When software is to be used on a disk sharing system, efforts will be made to secure this software from copying.

4. Illegal copies of copyrighted programs may not be made or used on school equipment.

5. The legal or insurance protection of the District will not be extended to employees who violate copyright laws.

6. _____ of this school district is designed as the only individual who may sign license agreements for software for schools in the district. (Each school using the software also should have a signature on a copy of the software agreement for local control.)

7. The principal of each school site is responsible for establishing practices which will enforce this policy at the school level.

ATTACHMENT 2
Sample Software Policy of a Community College with a Large Microcomputer Lab

It is the policy of this college that no person shall use or cause to be used in the college's microcomputer laboratories any software which does not fall into one of the following categories:

1. It is in the public domain.

2. It is covered by a licensing agreement with the software author, authors, vendor or developer, whichever is applicable.

3. It has been donated to the college and a written record of a bona fide contribution exists.

4. It has been purchased by the college and a record of bona fide purchase exists.

5. It has been purchased by the user and a record of a bona fide purchase exists and can be produced by the user upon demand.

6. It is being reviewed or demonstrated by the users in order to reach a decision about possible future purchase or request for contribution or licensing.

7. It has been written or developed by _____ (college employee) for the specific purpose of being used in the

_____ (college) microcomputer laboratory.

It is also the policy of the college that there be no copying of copyrighted or proprietary programs on computers belonging to the college.

Source: De Anza College, Cupertino, California.

ATTACHMENT 3
Suggested Format of Software Licenses

1. Designated on a per site, district-wide or other geographic basis.
2. Requires the signature of a responsible school employee.
3. Includes provisions for a single copy purchase (with archival back-up copy) at full price.
4. Multiple-machine pricing:
   Includes provisions for a quantity discount for subsequent purchases of the same software provided:
   a. the purchase discount applies to a single purchase order.
   b. the purchase discount is noncumulative.
   c. the software is for the same computer type.
   i.e.: Radio Shack presently offers a 50 percent discount for purchases of 10 or more sets of the same software; Gregg/McGraw-Hill offers a discount schedule with incremental increases — buy 2, pay 10 percent less; 3 — 20 percent less; 4 — 30 percent less; 5 or more, 40 percent less.
5. Network Pricing:
   May be offered as per school site or with quantity discount for school districts with multiple sites.
   Provide for a flat license fee for network-compatible versions of the software.
   - flat fee provision is preferred over any variable rate based on number of computers or number of student users.
   - network-compatibility, not just an unlocked version of the software, is required to eliminate the need for local reprogramming of copyrighted and licensed software.
   Include provision for purchase of multiple copies of documentation and accompanying materials.
   i.e.: A flat fee of two times the single copy retail price is offered to network users of Random House software.

ATTACHMENT 4
Some Technical Notes on
Software Encryption for Software/Hardware Vendors

1. Single Machine Encryption

Explanation: The purchased disk is not copiable by ordinary means. The software cannot be transferred to a network system or used on several computers at once. This scheme is the most common, especially for inexpensive software.

Technical notes: The protected disk is usually formatted in a nonstandard way which will defeat standard disk copy programs such as COPYA on the Apple or TRSDOS BACKUP on the TRS-80. Alternatively, the publisher may write special information on the disk in places which the standard disk copy programs do not check. The copy program proceeds to completion, but the special information is not transferred to the duplicate disk. When the duplicate is used, the software checks for the special information, fails to find it, and stops.

Implications: Schools will need to purchase many copies of the same program and should expect significant volume discounts. The customer is entitled to an archival back-up and should expect the publisher to include a back-up disk with every purchase.

Manufacturers of network systems should recognize that single machine encryption (which is incompatible with their products) will remain the software industry standard unless they actively support software protection on their systems.

2. Single Site Encryption

Explanation: A single product can serve all the machines at a site. This scheme applies to VisiCalc™ and Logo.

Technical Notes: Software which loads initially into memory and subsequently interacts only with data disks is de facto "single site encrypted," even though the program disk may be uncopiable. A single program disk can be used to initialize all the computers in a room, after which each user operates with his or her own data disks. VisiCalc™ and Logo operate in this way.

A functionally equivalent alternative is referred to as "master and slave" or "lock and key" encryption. This scheme is common where a program is too large to fit in memory all at once. Frequent disk access is needed as different parts of the software are brought into play.

In the "lock and key" scheme, the program modules which are routinely needed can be freely copied. A "slave" disk containing these modules is duplicated for each computer (or even for each student). The slave will not operate, however, unless the computer has been cold started with the (uncopiable) master disk.

Implications: Since the "master" disk is uncopiable, the publisher still bears the burden of providing an archival back-up. The protection on the "master" disk normally makes the software incompatible with network systems, so the above comments again apply.

Single site encryption reduces the dependence on volume discounts to facilitate multiple machine use. However, volume discounts should still be made available at the district level to encourage district level adoption of software.

3. Hard Disk/Network Compatible Versions of Software

Explanation: Floppy disks containing network compatible software must be copiable since the software is copied as it is transferred onto the network. The problem of protecting network compatible software is how to allow this legitimate copying while preventing illegal copying.

One solution is to abandon software protection altogether and to rely on license agreements to prevent illegal use of the program(s). The problem with this solution is that freely copiable software may be freely copied.

Other solutions rely on publishing special versions of the software for the various network systems available. These versions do not run on stand-alone computers.

A publisher can also take steps to discourage people from installing the network software at sites other than the intended site.

Technical Notes: A publisher can prevent network software from running on a stand-alone computer by using a device check. The software senses whether it is running on a network system and stops if it is not. The device check is specific to the network system involved. Software with a device check could be installed at many network sites, not just the one for which it was licensed.

To discuss use at non-licensed sites, the publisher can embed the name of the licensee in the software. This requires that the publisher customize each network-compatible version sold. Although such customization discourages porting the software to another network site, it does not physically prevent it.

To prevent porting of the software to another network, the publisher might implement what is essentially single machine encryption on the network level. This protection scheme would work by checking the serial number or other unique identifier in the network hardware. If the software encountered a change in identifier, it would fail to operate. This has the disadvantages that a licensee would have to be a single network installation and that normal activities such as replacing or upgrading one's network system would disable the software.

Implications: Use of a device or serial number check requires a publisher to maintain a separate inventory item for each devide to be supported. The time required for a publisher to embed the customer's name in each product sold for use on networks can become prohibitive.

These protection schemes may prove economically unfeasible for inexpensive software.

These protection schemes require close working relationships and sharing of information between publishers and network system manufacturers.

International Council for Computers in Education (ICCE),
University of Oregon, 1787 Agate Street, Eugene OR 97403.

Appendix E
Public Law 96–517
(Computer Amendment)
December 12, 1980

Copyright Law Amended Regarding Computer Programs

The following excerpt amending title 17, United States Code, is taken from Public Law 96–517, dated December 12, 1980 (94 STAT. 3028–29).

Sec. 10. (a) Section 101 of title 17 of the United States Code is amended to add at the end thereof the following new language:

"A 'computer program' is a set of statements or instructions to be used directly or indirectly in a computer in order to bring about a certain result."

(b) Section 117 of title 17 of the United States Code is amended to read as follows:

"§117. Limitations on exclusive rights: Computer programs

"Notwithstanding the provisions of section 106, it is not an infringement for the owner of a copy of a computer program to make or authorize the making" of another copy or adaptation of that computer program provided:

"(1) that such a new copy or adaptation is created as an essential step in the utilization of the computer program in conjunction with a machine and that it is used in no other manner, or

"(2) that such new copy or adaptation is for archival purposes only and that all archival copies are destroyed in the event that continued possession of the computer program should cease to be rightful.

"Any exact copies prepared in accordance with the provisions of this section may be leased, sold, or otherwise transferred, along with the copy from which such copies were prepared, only as part of the lease, sale, or other transfer of all rights in the program. Adaptations so prepared may be transferred only with the authorization of the copyright owner."

Appendix F

Guidelines for the
Proviso of Subsection 108(g)(2)
(Photocopying —
Interlibrary Arrangements)

1. As used in the proviso of subsection 108(g)(2), the words, "… such aggregate quantities as to substitute for a subscription to or purchase of such work" shall mean:

    (a) with respect to any given periodical (as opposed to any given issue of a periodical), filled requests of a library or archives (a "requesting entity") within any calendar year for a total of six or more copies of an article or articles published in such periodical within five years prior to the date of the request. These guidelines specifically shall not apply, directly or indirectly, to any request of a requesting entity for a copy or copies of an article or articles published in any issue of a periodical, the publication date of which is more than five years prior to the date when the request is made. These guidelines do not define the meaning, with respect to such a request, of "… such aggregate quantities as to substitute for a subscription to [such periodical]."

    (b) With respect to any other material described in subsection 108(d), (including fiction or poetry), filled requests of a requesting entity within any calendar year for a total of six or more copies of phonorecords or from any given work (including a collective work) during the entire period when such material shall be protected by copyright.

2. In the event that a requesting entity
   (a) shall have in force or shall have entered an order for a subscription to a periodical, or
   (b) has within its collection, or shall have entered an order for a copy or phonorecord of any other copyrighted work, material from either category of which it desires to obtain by copy from another library or archives (the "supplying entity"), because the material to be copied is not reasonably available for use by the requesting entity itself, then the fulfillment of such request shall be treated as though the requesting entity made such copy from its own collection. A library or archives may request a copy or phonorecord from a supplying entity only under those circumstances where the requesting entity would have been able, under the provisions of section 108, to supply such copy from materials in its own collection.

3. No request for a copy or phonorecord of any material to which these guidelines apply may be fulfilled by the supplying entity unless such request is accompanied by a representation by the requesting entity that the request was made in conformity with these guidelines.

4. The requesting entity shall maintain records of all requests made by it for copies or phonorecords of any materials to which these guidelines apply and shall maintain records of the fulfillment of such requests, which records shall be retained until the end of the third complete calendar year after the end of the calendar year in which the respective request shall have been made.

5. As part of the review provided for in subsection 108(i), these guidelines shall be reviewed not later than five years from the effective date of this bill.

Final Report of the National Commission on New Technological Uses of Copyrighted Works (CONTU)
Washington, D.C.: U.S.G.P.O. July 31, 1978; pp. 136–137.

Appendix G
Sections 107 and 108 of the 1976 Copyright Act Regarding Fair Use and Reproduction by Libraries

107. Limitations on exclusive rights: Fair use

Notwithstanding the provisions of section 106, the fair use of a copyrighted work, including such use by reproduction in copies or phonorecords or by any other means specified by that section, for purposes such as criticism, comment, news reporting, teaching (including multiple copies for classroom use), scholarship, or research, is not an infringement of copyright. In determining whether the use made of a work in any particular case is a fair use the factors to be considered shall include —

  (1) the purpose and character of the use, including whether such use is of a commercial nature or is for nonprofit educational purposes;
  (2) the nature of the copyrighted work;
  (3) the amount and substantiality of the portion used in relation to the copyrighted work as a whole; and
  (4) the effect of the use upon the potential market for or value of the copyrighted work.

108. Limitations on exclusive rights: Reproduction by libraries and archives.

(a) Notwithstanding the provisions of section 106, it is not an infringement of copyright for a library or archives, or any of its employees acting within the scope of their employment, to reproduce no more than one copy or phonorecord of a work, or to distribute such copy or phonorecord, under the conditions specified by this section, if —

    (1) the reproduction or distribution is made without any purpose of direct of indirect commercial advantage;

    (2) the collections of the library or archives are (i) open to the public, or (ii) available not only to researchers affiliated with the library or archives or with the institution of which it is a part, but also to other persons doing research in a specialized field; and

    (3) the reproduction or distribution of the work includes a notice of copyright.

(b) The rights of reproduction and distribution under this section apply to a copy or phonorecord of an unpublished work duplicated in facsimile form solely for purposes of preservation and security or for deposit for research use in another library or archives of the type described by clause (2) of subsection (a), if the copy or phonorecord reproduced is currently in the collections of the library or archives.

(c) The right of reproduction under this section applies to a copy or phonorecord of a published work duplicated in facsimile form solely for the purpose of replacement of a copy or phonorecord that is damaged, deteriorating, lost, or stolen, if the library or archives has, after a reasonable effort, determined that an unused replacement cannot be obtained at a fair price.

(d) The rights of reproduction and distribution under this section apply to a copy, made from the collection of a library or archives where the user makes his or her request or from that of another library or archives, of no more than one article or other contribution to a copyrighted collection or periodical issue, or to a copy or phonorecord of a small part of any other copyrighted work, if —

    (1) the copy or phonorecord becomes the property of the user, and the library or archives has had no notice that the copy or phonorecord would be used for any purpose other than private study, scholarship, or research; and

    (2) the library or archives displays prominently, at the place where orders are accepted, and includes on its order form, a warning of copyright in accordance with requirements that the Register of Copyrights shall prescribe by regulation.

(e) The rights of reproduction and distribution under this section apply to the entire work, or to a substantial part of it, made from the collection of a library or archives where the user makes his or her request or from that of another library or archives, if the library or archives has first determined, on the basis of a reasonable investigation, that a copy or phonorecord of the copyrighted work cannot be obtained at a fair price, if —

    (1) the copy or phonorecord becomes the property of the user, and the library or archives has had no notice that the copy or phonorecord would be used for any purpose other than private study, scholarship, or research; and

    (2) the library or archives displays prominently, at the place where orders are accepted, and includes on its order form, a warning of copyright in accordance with requirements that the Register of Copyrights shall prescribe by regulation.

(f) Nothing in this section —

    (1) shall be construed to impose liability for copyright infringement upon a library or archives or its employees for the unsupervised use of reproducing equipment located on its premises: *Provided*, That such equipment displays a notice that the making of a copy may be subject to the copyright law;

    (2) excuses a person who uses such reproducing equipment or who requests a copy or phonorecord under subsection (d) from liability for copyright infringement for any such act, or for any later use of such copy or phonorecord, if it exceeds fair use as provided by section 107;

    (3) shall be construed to limit the reproduction and distribution by lending of a limited number of copies and excerpts by a library or archives of an audiovisual news program, subject to clauses (1), (2), and (3) of subsection (a); or

    (4) in any way affects the right of fair use as provided by section 107, or any contractual obligations assumed at any time by the library or archives when it obtained a copy or phonorecord of a work in its collections.

(g) The rights of reproduction and distribution under this section extend to the isolated and unrelated reproduction or distribution of a single copy or phonorecord of the same material on separate occasions, but do not extend to cases where the library or archives, or its employee —

(1) is aware or has substantial reason to believe that it is engaging in the related or concerted reproduction or distribution of multiple copies or phonorecords of the same material, whether made on one occasion or over a period of time, and whether intended for aggregate use by one or more individuals or for separate use by the individual members of a group; or

(2) engages in the systematic reproduction or distribution of single or multiple copies or phonorecords of material described in subsection (d): *Provided*, That nothing in this clause prevents a library or archives from participating in interlibrary arrangements that do not have, as their purpose or effect, that the library or archives receiving such copies or phonorecords for distribution does so in such aggregate quantities as to substitute for a subscription to or purchase of such work.

(h) The rights of reproduction and distribution under this section do not apply to a musical work, a pictorial, graphic or sculptural work, or a motion picture or other audiovisual work other than an audiovisual work dealing with news, except that no such limitations shall apply with respect to rights granted by subsections (b) and (c), or with respect to pictorial or graphic works published as illustrations, diagrams, or similar adjuncts to works of which copies are reproduced or distributed in accordance with subsections (d) and (e).

(i) Five years from the effective date of this Act, and at five-year intervals thereafter, the Register of Copyrights, after consulting with representatives of authors, book and periodical publishers, and other owners of copyrighted materials, and with representatives of library owners of copyrighted materials, and with representatives of library users and librarians, shall submit to the Congress a report setting forth the extent to which this section has achieved the intended statutory balancing of the rights of creators, and the needs of users. The report should also describe any problems that may have arisen, and present legislative or other recommendations, if warranted.

Appendix H
Comments of the
American Library Association

on the Report of the
Register of Copyrights to Congress:

Library Reproduction
of Copyrighted Works

(17 U.S.C. 108) January 1983

What is the Register's Report?

Section 108 (i) of the Copyright Act of 1976, Title 17 United States Code, mandates that the Register of Copyrights transmit to Congress every five years a report setting forth the extent to which Section 108 "Reproduction by libraries and archives" has achieved "the intended statutory balancing of the rights of creators, and the needs of users."

The Act provides as follows:

"Section 108. Limitations on exclusive rights: Reproduction by libraries and archives.

(i) Five years from the effective date of this Act, and at five-year intervals thereafter, the Register of Copyrights, after consulting with representatives of authors, book and periodical publishers, and other owners of copyrighted materials, and with representatives of library users and librarians, shall submit to the Congress a report setting forth the extent to which this section has achieved the intended statutory balancing of the rights of creators, and the needs of users. The report should also describe any problems that may have arisen, and present legislative or other recommendations, if warranted."

The Register points out in his Introduction:

"The focus of this report, therefore, is not only on the rights of creators but principally on the practices of libraries, archives, and their users. It is concerned only incidentally with the enormous quantity of copying that takes place elsewhere, outside libraries, often in multiple copies, by private persons, business enterprises, government agencies, and educational and eleemosynary institutions. Attention is here fixed on the copying practices of libraries and archives, and only certain kinds of libraries or archives, and their clients."

What is the Register's point of view regarding the effectiveness of the Copyright Act of 1976 in maintaining a balance between the rights of creators and the users' needs for access?

The Register says:

"The short answer to the question of balance is that Sec. 108, with the rest of the Copyright Act of 1976, provides a workable structural framework for obtaining a balance between creators' rights and users' needs. Considering the complexity of the issues, the intensity of the controversies, the scope of the interests, and the rapid changes in technology before and after enactment, that is a remarkable achievement. In certain instances, however, the balance has not been achieved in practice, either because the intent of Congress has not been carried out fully or because that intent is not clear at all to the parties whose behavior lies within the ambit of the law. In some cases those deficiencies of the system in practice are serious. The threshold question, however, is: What is the balance?...

As a predicate for that answer, no quantification of "balance" is found in the statute. What is meant here by "balance" is whether Section 108, dealing with "reproduction by libraries and archives," allows users to use—by means of copying—works protected by copyright in a way both consistent with traditional principles of copyright law and library practice and not exceeding a minimal encroachment upon the rights of authors and copyright owners ...

The question whether a balance exists between the rights of creators and the needs of users ultimately turns not only on what the copyright law says but also on how people whose behavior is within the ambit of that law—here, chiefly, librarians and library patrons—actually do behave. A law which sets out to strike a balance between *any* conflicting claims must be assessed ultimately by whether the conduct of the persons within its ambit can fairly be said to comport with the behavior intended by Congress. In the case of library photocopying, the balance between creators and users is a function not simply of how librarians behave under the provisions of Section 108, but of how the tension between the rights of creators and the needs of library patrons is (or is not) resolved. This larger question requires one to look at *all* photocopying of library materials for their own or other libraries' collections, copies made by librarians for permanent transfer to patrons in their own or other libraries, and copies made by patrons for themselves, their colleagues, students, friends, or employers.

When discussing these issues of balance the use of correct terminology is of primary importance. For nearly a century libraries have engaged in a practice known as "interlibrary loan," wherein materials in the collection of one library are made available to patrons in another. When this is done by *lending* a printed (or other authorized) copy of a work to the "receiving" library on a temporary basis, the appellation *loan* is clearly correct and informative. When, however, this is done by making a photocopy (without the copyright owner's permission) which is then permanently transferred, by gift or by sale, to the receiving library or its patron, *loan* is at least imprecise.

Libraries have traditionally lent materials with no concern for the copyright law. This strong tradition may well account for the continued use of the term to describe a transaction which in no way resembles a loan. The distortion created by such misuse is that one may easily ignore the profound change in the role of libraries effected by the growth of photocopying. Data discussed in Chapter 5 of this show that among the library patrons surveyed, between one-fifth and one-quarter had asked libraries to obtain for them works from the collections of other libraries (which, when delivered, were often in the form of photocopies), and roughly three-fifths of the patrons interviewed upon entering libraries had made or obtained photocopies of library materials in the preceding six months. For a significant portion of the library user community, the library has become the location for *acquisition* of as well as *access* to, copyrighted materials. This phenomenon, which has been styled "republishing" should not be glossed over by calling some photocopying transactions "loans" when they are not.",...

The Register points out on page 2 of his report that "balance" can be seen in much of the evidence contained in the record upon which this report is based, and in the following broad statements based on that evidence:

- Between 1976 and 1980 library acquisition expenditures increased faster than the rate of inflation with larger real increases in serial than in book expenditures.
- During the same period, the ratio of serial 'births' to 'deaths' was 3.4 to 1, and the real increase in serial publishers' revenues was between 40 percent and 50 percent.
- There is some indication that some types of photocopying in certain classes of libraries have increased very slowly or even decreased during that time.
- Most librarians appear to believe that because of these factors the present system strikes an appropriate balance.

He then adds his own caveat to the above evidence: "Thus, some may surmise that all is well. There is, however, credible evidence that present conditions call this conclusion into doubt." He then lists three conditions as follows:

- Substantial quantities of the photocopies prepared by and for library patrons are made for job-related reasons, rather than for the type of private scholarship, study, or research most favored by the law.
- There appears to be significant confusion among many librarians about how the law works and why its enforcement is frequently *their* responsibility.
- Some publishers declare strongly that they believe the present system is seriously unbalanced. Their efforts, both in asserting their positions and in bringing lawsuits, demonstrate the seriousness of their concerns.

ALA says:

We agree with the Register's analysis that the Copyright Act of 1976 provides "a workable structural framework for obtaining a balance between creators' rights and users' needs" but *we disagree with his statement that a balance has not been achieved*. We believe that

users now have, under the new Copyright Law, access to materials
without exceeding the rights of copyright holders provided in the law.
We contend, therefore, that a balance has been achieved.

We take exception to the Register's constant referral in his report
to "creator's *rights'* and users' *needs.*" It is important to keep in mind
that both the creators and the users have certain "rights." The rights of
the copyright proprietors are granted by acts of Congress, not by the
Constitution itself, and accordingly are sometimes referred to as
statutory privileges. Users of copyrighted materials also have rights,
and these do originate in the Constitution. In particular, the First and
Ninth Amendments guarantee to the American people the right to
know and the right to read.

In United States law, copyright is a limited statutory monopoly
which involves the privilege to restrict as well as to monopolize the
diffusion of knowledge; hence, the public's *right* to use materials must
be protected. The late Chief Justice Charles Evans Hughes, in inter-
preting the copyright law, rendered the opinion: "The sole interest of
the United States and the primary object in conferring the monopoly lie
in the general benefit derived by the public from the labors of authors."

Certain safeguards have been written into the new law to protect
librarians, researchers, teachers and scholars as they carry out their
responsibilities for educating all the people or for conducting research.
Section 108 is one of the safeguards written into the law to enable
libraries and librarians to carry out the responsibilities for which they
are employed.

ALA's position is that the fundamental purpose of copyright is to
ensure use. The principal justification for providing a privilege for
creators is to guarantee use and access to materials in the public
interest. The whole history of the copyright law in the United States
exemplifies the fact that an author has no constitutional property right
in or to copyright protection and that such right as an author obtains is
a privilege to be granted or withheld by Congress in its discretion.

In reply to the Register's charge that librarians are "republishers,"
ALA Executive Director Robert Wedgeworth replies:

> We are not (republishers). We are lenders. The fact is that in
> many cases photocopying machines do not even pay their own
> way in libraries but must be subsidized out of tight library bud-
> gets. But if such machines were not made available in libraries,
> patrons desiring to copy even a page could either check out the
> entire work and take it to a copying machine elsewhere or sit

down and laboriously copy the page by hand—a practice common 20 years ago. Worse, some might rip out the pages they desire and prevent any further access to the information for any user.

Librarians are information providers. The law as it stands already calls for as much statistical compilation and oversight as may properly be required without jeopardizing library service. (See ALA testimony before the Copyright Office January 31, 1981 in Appendix Vol. VI, p. 65f.)

What is the relationship between Section 107 and Section 108?

The Register says:

"The dispute between the proprietary and library communities about the exact meaning or intent behind certain words and phrases in Section 108 are not the only important areas of disagreement. An overarching issue involves the broader (and harder) question about the relationship of Section 107 in which the doctrine of 'fair use' is now codified, to Section 108, in which 'special' rules governing certain libraries are set out....

The most accurate answer (to the above question) is the lawyers' commonplace: 'It depends.' The Copyright Office does not believe that Congress intended that there should *never* be fair use photocopying 'beyond' Section 108. On certain infrequent occasions, such copying may be permitted. But fair use privileges are not available on a broad and recurring basis once the copying permitted by Section 108 has occurred. Section 108 was enacted to make lawful some types of copying which would otherwise be infringements of copyright, fair use notwithstanding. This means that much '108' photocopying would be infringing but for the existence of that section, thus leaving Section 107 often clearly unavailable as a legal basis for photocopying not authorized by Section 108."

In a footnote on p. 96, the Register points out that the House Report states that "Section 108 authorizes certain photocopying practices which may not qualify as a fair use" (H. Rept. 94–1476 at p. 74). He adds, "Indeed, the library community sought section 108 to permit copying that had not been spelled out in the proposed fair use provision.... The Statutes strongly suggest that Section 108 exists to create immunity from infringement liability for copying that is *not* fair use, since to hold otherwise would be to render Section 108 superfluous.

The Register's Report recommends "that any analysis of the relationship between Sections 107 and 108 be carried out not on broad
theoretical grounds but on a case-by-case basis. The analysis should be
guided by a few clear principles:

1. That Section 108 was enacted to exempt certain non-fair use
   library photocopying from copyright liability.
2. That Section 108(f)(4) states that fair use is not affected by Section 108 (Section 108[f][4] states: 'Nothing in this section ... in
   any way affects the right of fair use as provided by Section
   107 ...').
3. That a fair use examination of a photocopying transaction
   'beyond' Section 108 *must* be made with due consideration for
   the fact that '108' copying privileges have already been exhausted."

The Register then adds: "To read Section 108 (f)(4) as permitting
'post-108' reliance on fair use *as if no Section 108 copying had occurred*
is to come dangerously close to reading Section 108 out of the statute....
The better position is that library photocopying 'beyond' 108 may be
fair use if *both*:

1. the transaction is of a *type* which could be fair use in the absence of Section 108, *and*
2. the fair use analysis (conducted only if [a] applies) of *this* transaction takes into account the '108' copying which had already
   occurred."

In short, the Register maintains that libraries are exhausting their
rights under Section 108 (which provides for single copying and up to
five copies from a single title of a periodical through interlibrary loan)
and then are using Section 107 as a back-up when the libraries have
exceeded the five copies allowed under the CONTU guidelines.

ALA says:

Congress disposed of the matter concerning the relationship of
Sections 107 and 108 in H. Rept. 94-1476, pp. 78-79:

> Nothing in Section 108 impairs the applicability of the fair use
> doctrine to a wide variety of situations involving photocopying
> or other reproduction by a library of copyrighted materials in its
> collections, where the user requests the reproduction for legiti-
> mate scholarly or research purposes ... (See Section 108 [f][4]).

There can be no better or clearer statement of the law. Rights of fair use
granted under Section 107 are independent of and not limited by those
rights granted under Section 108. Any other interpretation would

render superfluous the language of Subsection (f)(4) of Section 108, which provides that nothing in Section 108 "in any way affects the right of fair use as provided by Section 107 ..."

An understanding of the independence between the two sections is a tremendously important concept since it underlies two other points that ALA would like to make. First, the CONTU Guidelines, useful though they may be, are not, in any sense, inviolate rules. Second, if the Copyright Clearance Center (CCC) has not attracted the volume of use its creators expected, it is not as the publishers suggest, because libraries have engaged in wholesale illegal copying. Instead, there is strong evidence of several reasons CCC reports low use. The first problem is that CCC's jurisdiction and its services are limited. Of the 200,000 serials extant, CCC had jurisdiction for only some 6,500 as of June 1983. More important for interlibrary loan purposes is the fact that CCC has no collection of journals itself from which to provide copies. And the most important reason of all is that only a small percentage of library copying falls outside the limits of fair use. This is the conclusion supported by much of the testimony received from librarians across the country who have worked with the law and fair use guidelines and who testified before the Copyright Office during its hearings in 1980.

In reply to the Register's statement that libraries are exhausting their rights under Section 108 and then using Section 107 as a back-up when they have exceeded the five copies allowed under the CONTU guidelines, ALA points out that librarians rely on Section 107 only in unusual circumstances. A case in point would be when a library visitor may come in with an unusual one-time-only request for several articles for research purposes. The purpose of the CONTU guidelines is to help define the point at which a library could properly be expected to expand its collection into an area of new interest. More specifically, the guidelines define the parameters of a safe harbor; certainly, if there are only four requests for articles from a specialized chemical journal, a library should not be expected to expand its collection and subscribe. The librarian is then left to develop a reasonable approach beyond the actual guidelines. It seems clear, for instance, that six requests would in many cases constitute cause for subscribing to the publication. But if one user came into a public library and asked for 11 articles from a single journal title from which that library had never had another request and probably never will again, logic and reasonableness would not dictate that the library subscribe to that publication. There is no evidence that increasing restrictions on this type of library photocopying would have any other result than a decrease in the availability of certain materials to libraries and users, including authors, without any gain to the publishers.

Furthermore, the educational fair use guidelines for books and periodicals which are included in H. Rept. 94-1476, pp. 68-70, specifically state in the preamble that the purpose of the guidelines is to state the *minimum and not the maximum* standards of educational fair use under Section 107. The preamble continued: "There may be instances in which copying which does not fall within the guidelines ... may nonetheless be permitted under the criteria of fair use." The same standard holds true in the case of the music guidelines and the CONTU guidelines. In the final analysis, librarians must be responsible for evaluating each new situation in light of the letter and spirit of the copyright law.

With regard to reserve room use, ALA with advice of legal counsel and academic librarians, developed a model policy ("Model Policy Concerning College and University Photocopying for Classroom Research and Library Reserve Use," ALA, March 1982). It asserts that at the request of a faculty member a library may photocopy materials in its collection for reserve room use for the convenience of students both in preparing class assignments and in pursuing informal educational activities which higher education requires, such as advanced independent study and research. A reasonable number of copies will in most instances be less than six, but factors such as the length or difficulty of the assignment, the number of enrolled students and the length of time allowed for completion of the assignment may permit more in unusual circumstances.

Copyright Office Recommendations

In Chapter IX of the Register's Report, the Copyright Office—in keeping with its mandate by Congress in title 17 of the *U.S. Code*, Sec. 108 (1)—summarizes seven non-statutory recommendations and five statutory recommendations which represent their "best judgment" about possible solutions to the copyright issues relating to library reproduction of copyrighted works based upon:

1. consultation with representatives of authors, book and periodical publishers and other owners of copyrighted materials, and with representatives of library users and librarians about

their understandings of, and experience under, the Copyright Act, and their proposed solutions, if any;

2. the surveys of library reproduction of works, of publishers, and of users reported by King Research, Inc., under contract with the Copyright Office;

3. a review of library reproduction abroad and of the technological developments affecting library reproduction of works; and

4. a review of the text and legislative history of the pertinent sections of the Copyright Act.

The non-statutory and statutory recommendations of the Copyright Office are listed below, followed by a brief reaction to each one by ALA:

A. *Non-statutory Recommendations*

1. *Collective licensing arrangements encouraged*
   "All parties affected by library reproduction of copyrighted works are encouraged to participate in existing collective licensing arrangements, and to develop new collective arrangements to facilitate compensated copying of copyrighted works."
   ALA's Reaction:
   ALA has several reservations about collective licensing systems —
   a. They tend to erode fair use.
   b. They are not mandatory on all copyright owners.
   c. They would be subject to escalating fees.
   d. They would not cover all types of materials.
   e. They would be difficult to administer.
   f. They usually exclude representation of user interests in the control of the system.

2. *Voluntary guidelines encouraged*
   "Representatives of authors, publishers, librarians and users should engage in serious discussions with a view to clarification of terms and development of guidelines, both with respect to present photocopying practices and the impact of new technological developments on library use of copyrighted works."
   ALA's Reaction:
   ALA feels the present photocopying guidelines are adequate and are working well. The CONTU Guidelines are useful guides, but

they do not carry the force of the law. They do not purport to set maximum limits on library photocopying practices but strive only to establish a safe harbor. They should not be allowed to become firm rules which may cause librarians unnecessarily to deny their patrons' rights. ALA supports the Register's recommendation for the development of voluntary guidelines covering the use of the new technologies and their impact on library use of copyrighted works. We urge that representatives of technological software and hardware groups be included in these discussions, as was the case in the development of the Off-Air Taping Guidelines for Education Use.

It should be pointed out, however, that soon guidelines will be more voluminous than the law. There will always be situations which will arise that will be outside the guidelines. This is inevitable but that is where the four fair use principles should be relied upon.

3. *Study of surcharge on equipment*
"In the next five-year review, a copyright compensation scheme based upon a surcharge on photocopying equipment used at certain locations and in certain types of institutions or organizations should be studied, taking into account experience with such systems in other countries."
ALA's Reaction:
ALA recommends that no action be taken on this recommendation until the Supreme Court has rendered its decision on the Betamax case and until Congress has made its determination on the legislation now pending on home video recording. Furthermore, most uses of these machines have nothing to do with copyright!

4. *Study of compensation systems based on sampling techniques*
"In the next five-year review, various systems for copyright compensation based on a percentage of the photocopying impressions made on machines located at certain places in certain types of institutions or organizations, as determined by sampling techniques, should be studied."
ALA's Reaction:
ALA opposes this recommendation because of the cost of administering such a system. This would require spending too much money to obtain little or no benefit. Judging from previous studies

aimed at developing royalty systems of one type or another, no equitable method of distribution of proceeds is likely to be devised that would satisfy all proprietary groups. Again, this would be spending dollars to collect nickels and dimes.

5. *Further study of new technology issues*

"In the next five-year review, issues relating to the impact of new technological developments on library use of copyrighted works should be studied."

ALA's Reaction:

ALA heartily supports this recommendation. In fact, at a public hearing before the Copyright Office, Library of Congress, on January 28, 1981, the ALA—in the testimony presented by Robert Wedgeworth, Executive Director of ALA—proposed discussions on electronic distribution of copyrighted materials. Wedgeworth stated: "Publishers and authors should join librarians in planning how the electronic networks can be structured to support publishing and authorship, while providing users with greater access to published works through libraries and other agencies."

6. *Archival preservation*

"Representatives of authors, publishers, users, and librarians should meet to review fully new preservation techniques and their copyright implications and should seek to develop a common position for legislative action by Congress, taking into account the respective interests of libraries and their patrons and of authors and publishers."

ALA's Reaction:

ALA supports this recommendation.

7. *Adequate funding for library services*

"Proper recognition of the cost of creating and disseminating protected works in our society requires concomitant understanding at all levels of government of the need for adequate funding of publicly owned libraries to enable them to pay their share of creation-dissemination costs."

ALA's Reaction:

Obviously, the library community supports this recommendation, but for a very different reason. Libraries already pay their share, and more, of creation-dissemination costs as vital links in the information chain; they consistently seek higher budgets for collection development; and the latest price indexes indicate that 70 percent of the serial titles covered in the index sample are available to libraries only at institutional prices which may be from 10 to 100 percent more than rates charged individuals.

B. *Statutory Recommendations*

2. *Reproduction of out-of-print musical works*
   "The Copyright Office recommends enactment of the proposal submitted by the Music Library Association and the Music Publishers' Association either by amendment of Section 108(e) or addition of a new paragraph (j) to Section 108, with consequential amendment of paragraph (h). If enacted, the amendment would permit library reproduction of an entire musical work (or substantial parts thereof) for private study, scholarship, or research following an unsuccessful, diligent search for the name and address of the copyright proprietor of the musical work."

ALA's Reaction:

While other members of the library community are sympathetic to the plight of music librarians and agree with the principle underlying the proposed change, we are concerned with the MLA/MPA approach in relation to Section 108(e) in that it places considerable emphasis on finding the *owner* (and presumably paying a copying fee) as opposed to finding a *copy* at a *fair price.* Further, it requires a diligent search for the proprietor which may go beyond a search of Copyright Office records, as opposed to "the normal situation," i.e., a search for the owner at the address listed on the Copyright Office registration. We would support an amendment which would delete the restrictions against musical works in Section 108(h) and include them under Section 108(e) rights.

2. *"Umbrella statute."*
   "The Copyright Office recommends favorable action by Congress on legislation embodying the principle of the so-called 'umbrella statute,' a proposal developed by an ad hoc task force of librarians [for-profit] and publishers and submitted by the Association of American Publishers. The proposal would add

a new section 511 to the Copyright Act limiting copyright owners to a single remedy—a reasonable copying fee—for copyright infringement of their scientific, technical, medical or business periodicals or proceedings, if certain conditions are met by the user of the work, including membership in a collective licensing arrangement, unless the work was entered in a qualified licensing system or qualified licensing program. The purpose of the 'umbrella statute' is to encourage publisher and user participation in collective licensing arrangements. The Copyright Office further recommends that Congress require recordation with the Office of a document setting forth the basic terms and conditions of any qualified licensing program or qualified licensing system."

ALA's Reaction:

The library community opposes such a statute because it requires mandatory registration by users in a collective licensing arrangement, such as the CCC, and the payment of a "single, reasonable fee" for copying protected works even if that copying fell under fair use provisions of the current statute. The proposed amendment to the statute is more complex than appears here, and, in our judgment, the concept is much too complicated to be administered effectively. It is no wonder, however, that the AAP proposed amendment attempts to encourage publisher participation in the CCC. King found that less than 5 percent of all U.S. publishers belong while 5.6 percent of libraries belong. ALA has stated that "The low incidence of use of the CCC is consistent with the overall decrease in photocopying, the high incidence of single-copy library reproduction (p. 3–30) [King Report], adherence to the CONTU Guidelines, and the willingness of so many publishers to grant permission without charge."

3. Clarification of the "108(a) notice."

"The Copyright Office recommends enactment of a clarifying amendment to section 108(a)(3) as follows:

(3) the reproduction or distribution of the work includes the notice of copyright as provided in sections 401 and 402 of this title, if such notice appears on the copy or phonorecord in a position authorized by sections 401(c) and 402(c), respectively, of this title.

Publishers have generally interpreted the present Copyright

Act as requiring libraries to use the statutory copyright notice on photocopies as a condition of Section 108 copying privileges. Librarians have generally disagreed, maintaining that a warning that a work may be in copyright complies with the Act. The Amendment would accept the publishers' interpretation."

ALA's Reaction:

ALA would oppose the enactment of such an amendment, unless publishers would agree to place the copyright notice on the initial page of an article or the verso of the title page of a book or monograph.

4. *Clarification that unpublished works are excluded from paragraphs (d) and (e) of Section 108.*

"The Copyright Office recommends an amendment to paragraphs (d) and (e) of Section 108 to make clear that unpublished works are not within the copying privileges granted therein. Section 108(d) governs single copying of a small part of a work or one article of a periodical; Section 108(e) establishes the conditions under which out-of-print works may be copied—either the entire work or a substantial part thereof. In the case of paragraph (d), the term 'published' should be inserted in lieu of the word 'copyrighted' each time the latter appears. In the case of paragraph (e), the term 'published' should be inserted between 'entire' and 'work' and should be inserted in lieu of the word 'copyrighted.' "

ALA's Reaction:

The library community needs to study this proposed amendment in greater depth in terms of educational scholarship and research.

5. *Change in reporting month for the Section 108(i) report*

"The Copyright Office recommends amendment of paragraph (i) of Section 108 to permit the filing of the periodic five-year report on or about March 1 of a given year in place of the present January reporting date. This change in the filing date is requested because of the staffing and administrative support problems inherent in preparing a major report during the year-end holiday period."

ALA's Reaction:

No comment.

Concluding Statement

Throughout the Register's Report the implication is made that librarians and the library community have engaged in copying that far exceeds the limits of the law. In his Executive Summary, the Register clearly points his finger at the library community as the cause of the imbalance he sees between the creator's rights and those of the user. At one point he strongly implies that librarians "have failed to comport with the behavior intended by Congress." Because of this, we feel the Report is heavily weighted on the side of proprietary groups and lacks balance and objectivity, despite massive amounts of statistical data in the King Research Report which is based on observation.

Librarians *are* complying with the law. Most photocopying done by libraries is within the bounds of Sections 107 and 108. Libraries utilize rights under both these sections to contribute to the widest possible dissemination of information to the public and to fulfill their traditional role in society as lenders and facilitators of such information.

Publishers should not view librarians as the "enemy" in a war over photocopy profits. Libraries do not reduce the size of their collections because of the availability of photocopies. Indeed, reliance on networking to substitute for a subscription to a periodical is not only illegal; it is inefficient and expensive. Every library strives to be as comprehensive in its collection development area as it can be. The availability of photocopies for the occasional user interested in an unusual field makes possible the kind of access to information so important to our society's very foundation.

Index